Wellington's Cavalry and Technical Corps, 1800–1815

Wellington's Cavalry and Technical Corps, 1800–1815

Including Artillery

Gabriele Esposito

Pen & Sword
MILITARY

First published in Great Britain in 2021
by Pen & Sword Military
An imprint of Pen & Sword Books Limited
47 Church Street
Barnsley
South Yorkshire
S70 2AS

ISBN 978 1 39900 547 0

A CIP catalogue record for this book is
available from the British Library

Typeset in Adobe Caslon
by Mac Style

Printed and bound in India by Replika Press Pvt. Ltd.

Pen & Sword Books Limited incorporates the imprints of Atlas,
Archaeology, Aviation, Discovery, Family History, Fiction, History, Maritime,
Military, Military Classics, Politics, Select, Transport, True Crime, Air World,
Frontline Publishing, Leo Cooper, Remember When, Seaforth Publishing,
The Praetorian Press, Wharncliffe Local History, Wharncliffe Transport,
Wharncliffe True Crime and White Owl.

For a complete list of Pen & Sword titles please contact
PEN & SWORD BOOKS LIMITED
47 Church Street, Barnsley, South Yorkshire, S70 2AS, England
E-mail: enquiries@pen-and-sword.co.uk
Website: www. pen-and-sword.co.uk

Contents

Gabriele Esposito is a military historian who works as a freelance author and researcher for some of the most important publishing houses in the military history sector. In particular, he is an expert specializing in uniformology: his interests and expertise range from the ancient civilizations to modern post-colonial conflicts. During recent years, he has conducted and published several researches on the military history of the Latin American countries, with special attention on the War of the Triple Alliance and the War of the Pacific. He is among the leading experts on the military history of the Italian Wars of Unification and the Spanish Carlist Wars. His books and essays are published on a regular basis by Osprey Publishing, Winged Hussar Publishing and Libreria Editrice Goriziana; he is also the author of numerous military history articles appearing in specialized magazines like *Ancient Warfare Magazine*, *Medieval Warfare Magazine*, *The Armourer*, *History of War*, *Guerres et Histoire*, *Focus Storia* and *Focus Storia Wars*.

Acknowledgements

This book is dedicated to my parents, Maria Rosaria and Benedetto, for the great love and fundamental advice that they have given me throughout my life. A very special thanks goes to Philip Sidnell, the commissioning editor of my books for Pen & Sword: his love for history and his passion for publishing are the key factors behind the success of our publications. A special mention goes to the production manager of this title, Matt Jones, for his great competence and patience. Last but not least, a special acknowledgement goes to Tony Walton, for the editing of this book with his usual passion and competence, as well as for honouring me with his sincere friendship. All the pictures published in this book are public domain ones obtained from the magnificent Digital Collections of the Brown University Library and the New York Public Library. Everyone with an interest in military history can easily browse the vast contents of the latter at: https://library.brown.edu/info/collections/askb/prints/https://digitalcollections.nypl.org/collections/the-vinkhuijzen-collection-of-military-uniforms#/?tab=navigation.

Introduction

The main aim of this book is to present a detailed overview of the organization, uniforms and equipments of the British mounted and technical corps that took part in the Napoleonic Wars. The period covered in this work coincides with one of the most glorious moments in the military history of Britain, during which the British Army fought around the globe to counter the expansionist ambitions of Napoleon and his newly established French Empire. After the Peace of Amiens was broken in 1803, Great Britain found itself at war with an old enemy (France) but also with a new competitor (Napoleon): the latter was the greatest military commander of his times, a man who was able to transform the French Army into the most lethal fighting machine of the early nineteenth century. The war experiences of 1793–1803 had not been positive ones for the British Army, which was still recovering from the crushing defeats suffered during the American War of Independence and badly needed to be reformed in order to become more efficient and modern. At the turn of the new century, Britain was still the greatest colonial power of the time and could count on the most formidable navy in the world; on land, however, its army was too weak to confront the French on anything like equal terms. The British land forces did not have a great leader comparable to Napoleon and were still influenced by tactical models that had been outclassed by the military events of the French Revolution. During the Napoleonic Wars, the British military apparatus did make attempts to improve, especially thanks to the guidance of a new generation of educated officers. These innovative and capable men reformed the British Army by improving its standards of service and creating a new relationship (based on mutual trust) with the men under their command. Wellington was the greatest of these officers, one of the few European generals who had the personal capabilities to effectively oppose Napoleon: it was he who forged the new British Army by fighting against the French in the Iberian Peninsula from 1808–1814. After learning from experience, British soldiers, aided by Dutch and Belgian allies and the Prussians, were able to face and decisively defeat Napoleon on the Belgian fields of Waterloo, thereby writing the last page of a glorious military epic. Waterloo, however, was just the final result of a long process. Between 1800 and 1815, British officers had to completely reform the tactical and operational patterns of their units. For example, it can be said that a 'light

From the left, trooper of the 2nd Life Guards, officer of the Horse Guards, officer of the 1st Life Guards and officers of the 2nd Life Guards. Except for the last figure that has M1812 dress, they are all wearing their M1797 uniform.

cavalry revolution' took place among the ranks of the mounted troops. All this was an experimental process, which sometimes led to bad results: the glorious actions of the Peninsula were not the only ones fought during this period. We should not forget the three largely disastrous campaigns conducted in the Netherlands (1799, 1809 and 1814) by the British Army.

To follow the evolution of the troop types taken into account here, we have divided the text into seven chapters. The first chapter will deal with the elite of the British cavalry, the three regiments of Life Guards and Horse Guards; the second one will analyse the general organization of the heavy cavalry, with its regiments of Guards Dragoons and Dragoons; the third will be devoted to light cavalry and will reconstruct the important 'light cavalry revolution' mentioned above; the fourth chapter will deal with the Royal Artillery and the other technical corps of the British Army; the fifth will cover two little-known categories of troops, the Yeomanry and the Fencibles, as well as the foreign units of cavalry and artillery that served with the British Army during the Napoleonic Period (including the formidable King's German Legion); the sixth chapter will reconstruct the organization of the cavalry and artillery units that were deployed in the various colonies of Britain; and the final one will briefly analyse the structure and functions of the Royal Marines and the Sea Fencibles. The latter were part of the Royal Navy and not of the British Army, but they have been included in this book since they had a lot in common with Wellington's 'auxiliary' technical corps. All the chapters dedicated to the most important troop types will include descriptions of their uniforms and equipment.

Chapter 1

The Life Guards and the Horse Guards

History and organization

Like all the major European military forces of the Napoleonic Period, the British Army comprised several cavalry units that had 'guard' status. These acted as the mounted bodyguard of the royal family and were considered to be the elite of the British heavy cavalry. In 1800, there were three guard corps of the British mounted troops: the 1st Regiment of Life Guards, the 2nd Regiment of Life Guards and the Royal Horse Guards. The history of the Life Guards began in 1658, when England and Scotland were still two independent realms ruled by the same monarch; as a result, they were originally part of the English Army. A 1st Troop of Life Guards was raised in 1658 as part of the military forces organized from his most loyal followers by Charles II during his exile in the Spanish Netherlands. During the same year, the exiled Stuart monarch raised a 2nd Troop of Life Guards, with the official denomination of 'The Duke of York's Troop of Horse Guards'. A 3rd Troop of Life Guards was added in 1659, this being commonly known as 'Monck's Lifeguards', the nickname deriving from the fact that this unit acted as the mounted bodyguard of George Monck, the main political supporter of Charles II during his exile. The members of the three Lifeguard units were known as 'gentlemen', since they all came from the higher social classes of England, and were required to provide their own horses and uniforms. In 1660, with the Restoration of the monarchy, Charles II returned to England and regained his throne. Consequently, the Life Guards were absorbed into the reorganized English Army and continued to act as the mounted bodyguard of the king. In 1678, one company of horse grenadiers was added to each troop of Life Guards, made up of ordinary soldiers rather than 'gentlemen'.

During the last quarter of the seventeenth century, horse grenadiers became popular in European armies, together with their foot equivalents. Hand-grenades were at the time commonly used during pitched battles, being employed to destroy field fortifications built by the enemy. It soon became clear that the soldiers tasked with throwing hand-grenades during battles had to receive specific training; in addition, they had to be chosen from the tallest and fittest recruits of the various units. As a result, the best soldiers in each infantry company started to be trained and equipped in a specific way as grenadiers, and over time they were assembled into independent

Trooper of the 1st Life Guards with M1812 uniform.

companies or battalions and thus became a fixed new component of European armies. Around 1670, the first corps of horse grenadiers started to appear in various armies. These were not truly cavalry units, since their members acted as mounted infantrymen, using their horses to travel long distances but usually dismounting to fight. It was practically impossible, in fact, to throw hand-grenades from horseback.

With the addition of the three companies of horse grenadiers, the numerical establishment of the Horse Guards became significantly larger. The 'gentlemen' did not have a high opinion of their 'plebeian' comrades, although the latter provided an important tactical support to the traditional cavalry thanks to their peculiar weaponry. The internal composition of a troop of Life Guards was as follows: one captain, four lieutenants, one cornet, one guidon-bearer, one quartermaster, four brigadiers, four sub-brigadiers, four trumpeters, one kettledrummer and 200 'gentlemen'. The companies of horse grenadiers had two lieutenants, two sergeants, two corporals, two drummers, four hautboys (oboe players) and sixty-four privates. In 1686, a 4th Troop of Life Guards, with an attached company of horse grenadiers, was raised by James II as part of a larger expansion of the English Army. In addition to the four Life Guard units, which were all part of the English Army, there was also a Scottish corps of Life Guards, formed by Viscount Newburgh shortly after the Restoration of Charles II in 1661. Originally, the unit had an establishment with four officers, five NCOs, one surgeon, one clerk, three trumpeters, one kettledrummer and 120 troopers. A 2nd Troop of Scottish Life Guards was raised soon after the first, but had a very short history as it was disbanded in 1676. During James II's reign, Ireland also had an independent Troop of Life Guards, which had an attached company of grenadiers like their English equivalent. This was quartered in Dublin and was to act as the mounted bodyguard of the king when he was in Ireland.

With the outbreak of the Glorious Revolution and the landing of William of Orange in England, the internal organization of the Life Guards was changed in a significant way. The armies of England, Scotland and Ireland remained independent from each other, but the new English king rationalized their internal structure. The English 4th Troop of Life Guards, which had been recently formed by James II, was disbanded in 1689. During the following ten years, it was replaced by a foreign military unit from the Netherlands that was on English pay: the Garde du Corps. As William of Orange was also the ruler of the Netherlands, the invasion force with which he landed in England was mostly made up of Dutch military units. Being unsure of the loyalty of his new subjects, William retained several Dutch units on English pay long after the end of his Glorious Revolution. The Garde du Corps, also known as 4th Troop of Life Guards, returned to their homeland only in 1699. The Scottish Life Guards remained loyal to James II during the Glorious Revolution, and thus most of them resigned their positions. William, however, soon reorganized the unit with new 'gentlemen' who were loyal to his cause. The troop of Irish Life Guards, however, was permanently disbanded since its members followed James II into exile and continued to serve the deposed monarch in France (as part of his army in exile). In 1709, the English Army and the Scottish Army were merged in order to form the new British Army. Consequently, the Scottish Life Guards were assembled with their English equivalents and became the new 4th Troop of Life Guards. Meanwhile, in 1693, the three troops of English horse grenadiers had been assembled into a single unit known as Horse Grenadier Guards. These had the numerical establishment of a single troop but were completely independent from the 'gentlemen' of the Life Guards. In 1702, a troop of horse grenadiers was raised in Scotland and attached to the Scottish Life Guards; when the latter became part of the British Army in 1709, it was detached from its 'mother corps' and became an independent unit. As a result, the new British Army had a 1st and a 2nd Troop of Horse Grenadiers, in addition to the four troops of Life Guards.

From their foundation, the units of Life Guards had a distinct 'heavy cavalry' nature, which over time was also acquired by the troops of horse grenadiers, which abandoned the use of hand-grenades and became ordinary heavy cavalry units. In 1746, the 3rd and 4th Troop of Life Guards were disbanded, following the outbreak of the Jacobite Rebellion that ravaged Scotland. In 1788, as part of the great organizational changes that took place after the British military defeat in the American Revolution, it was decided to assemble the two remaining troops of Life Guards with the two troops of Horse Grenadiers in order to form two consolidated regiments: the 1st and 2nd Regiment of Life Guards. The former was created by combining the 1st Troop of Life Guards and the 1st Troop of Horse Grenadiers; the latter comprisedthe 2nd Troop of Life Guards and the 2nd Troop of Horse Grenadiers. With this important organizational change, the nature of the Life Guards changed; the two new regiments started to comprise ordinary soldiers and were no longer made up of young 'gentlemen' as they had been in the past. Most of the aristocrats who were still serving in the Life Guards were pensioned off; as a result, the two new units started to comprise common soldiers who had distinguished themselves for their valour and discipline.

Both the 1st and 2nd Regiment of Life Guards served with distinction during the Napoleonic Wars. In 1922, they were assembled into a single regiment, simply known as The Life Guards, which is still part of the British Army today. Until 1812, the Life Guards did not play an active part in the campaigns that were fought by Britain against Napoleon; in that year, however, they finally had the opportunity to show their valour in battle. Since their foundation in 1788, neither unit had ever participated in any military campaign conducted overseas. In 1812, the two

Trooper of the Horse Guards with M1812 uniform.

regiments were assembled into a Household Brigade and were sent to the Iberian Peninsula, where Wellington was fighting against the French at the head of a large portion of the British Army. After spending six months in Lisbon, performing only ceremonial duties and improving their combat training, the Household Brigade was finally employed against the French during 1813.

The Life Guards took part in the decisive Battle of Vittoria, which saw the defeat of Napoleon's brother Joseph Bonaparte and the fall of the latter's rule over Spain. In 1814, with the rest of the Peninsular Army, the Life Guards crossed the Pyrenees and invaded southern France. They participated in the Battle of Toulouse, but like some months before at Vittoria, they conducted no glorious charges against the enemy. Wellington preferred to employ his battle-hardened regiments of veterans instead of the relatively inexperienced guardsmen, who were generally kept in reserve during major engagements and continued to have few opportunities to show their valour. In 1815, with the return of Napoleon from exile on Elba, the Household Brigade was re-formed and sent to Belgium in order to stop the advance of the French. Again under Wellington's orders, the Life Guards played their part in the Battle of Waterloo. They finally had the opportunity to fight like all the other mounted regiments of the British Army. During the early phases of the battle, the 1st Regiment of Life Guards counter-charged the formidable lancers of Napoleon's Imperial Guard, an action that saved other British cavalry units from destruction and bolstered the martial spirit of the Life Guards. Later during the battle, the two regiments of Life Guards launched a successful massive charge against the French lines, routing enemy infantry units, capturing two French Eagles (Imperial standards), putting 15 enemy guns out of action and even reaching the French wagon train. The charge of the Life Guards was a key factor in Wellington's victory at Waterloo, but it should be noted that after breaking the French lines the British heavy cavalry lost their previous cohesion and experienced serious difficulties in returning to their starting position. Nevertheless, the Household Brigade had won its first laurels on the battlefield and finally shown the world that it had notable combat capabilities. During the following decades, it would again be employed as a true military corps and not just as a ceremonial force that was only seen during parades.

The Royal Horse Guards, commonly known as the Blues because of their distinctive dark blue uniforms, had a completely different history to the two regiments of Life Guards. In 1650, with Oliver Cromwell at the peak of his power, a heavy cavalry unit known as the Regiment of Cuirassiers was raised by Sir Arthur Haselrig. From the outset, this corps had a distinct 'elite' status and was mostly employed for escort and policing duties, performing more or less the same function as the later French Gendarmerie. With the Restoration of Charles II in 1660, the Regiment of Cuirassiers

Troopers of the 1st Life Guards (left) and the Horse Guards (right), both with M1812 dress.

was transferred to Royal service and most of its officers (who were still loyal to the Parliamentarist cause) were replaced by new ones who were loyal to the Stuarts. The unit initially consisted of just three troops, whose members were mostly wealthy gentlemen. By the outbreak of the Glorious Revolution, however, it had eight troops and had received the new official denomination of The King's Regiment of Horse. Shortly before the Glorious Revolution, the corps had received guard status, but when William of Orange disembarked in England, its members abandoned James II and sided with the Dutch pretender to the English throne. During the early decades of the eighteenth century, the regiment continued to serve mostly as a police corps, garrisoning several areas of Britain and preventing the outbreak of local rebellions. In 1743, as part of Britain's involvement in the Austrian War of Succession that ravaged continental Europe, the corps fought with distinction at the Battle of Dettingen. The British forces that were sent across the English Channel to fight against France comprised, for the first time, a Household Brigade made up of elements from the Life Guards and Horse Grenadiers, as well as the future Royal Horse Guards (at that time still simply known by the name of their commanding colonel). At Dettingen, the Household Brigade showed great discipline and courage but could do little to determine the outcome of the battle. In 1745, the Blues also fought at the Battle of Fontenoy, during which they suffered heavy casualties and could not prevent the defeat of the British forces.

In 1750, the Blues received their new official denomination of the Regiment of Royal Horse Guards, under which they fought in the Seven Years' War. During this conflict, the Blues distinguished itself in three important battles: Minden (1759), Warburg (1760) and Villinghausen (1761). When the regiment returned to Britain in 1763 at the end of hostilities, it had lost most of its best elements due to the heavy casualties suffered. As a result, the Royal Horse Guards had to be completely reorganized. In 1788, after spending several years patrolling the countryside of the East Midlands, the Royal Horse Guards were transferred to London as a result of the reorganization of the Life Guards. The government was unsure about the reliability of the new Regiments of Life Guards that had just been reorganized, and thus decided to deploy the Blues in the capital where they felt they could count on their experience. Until then, the Royal Horse Guards had mostly been employed to perform internal police duties, but had also seen substantial fighting overseas. In 1793, after the outbreak of war with Revolutionary France, the Blues were sent to continental Europe and took part in operations in the Flanders. Despite the many difficulties encountered, the Royal Horse Guards showed all their discipline and valour during this campaign. However, the Flanders campaign ended in failure for the British Army and their allies, with Belgium and the Netherlands finally occupied by the French.

New barracks were built for the Royal Horse Guards at Windsor in 1800, and the unit started to perform as a mounted bodyguard for the royal family on a permanent basis. However, the regiment only received the same elite status as the Life Guards in 1820. In 1812, the Blues became part of the Household Brigade together with the Life Guards, and were sent to the Iberian Peninsula. There, under Wellington, they participated in the Battle of Vittoria but were prevented from conducting a charge against the French by the morphology of the terrain. In 1814, along with the rest of the Peninsular army, the Royal Horse Guards returned to Britain, but were soon re-mobilized together with the other units of the Household Brigade due to Napoleon's return to France. The Blues participated with great distinction at the Battle of Waterloo, during which they fought successfully against the French heavy cavalry. In particular, the Royal Horse Guards counter-charged the French Cuirassiers, who were considered to be the best heavy cavalry in Europe. The Blues showed that they were second-to-none in terms of courage and discipline, thereby confirming their excellent reputation. In 1820, the Royal Horse Guards, like the Life Guards, received new uniforms with cuirasses, similar to the ceremonial dress still worn today. It should be noted, however, that they had already used (albeit for a brief period) metal cuirasses some years before. This happened in 1794, while the regiment was deployed on the continent to fight against the French, but they soon discarded their cuirasses as they were extremely uncomfortable to wear.

Generally speaking, the mounted regiments of the British Army were structured on troops, two of which made up a squadron. At the beginning of the Revolutionary Wars against France, the two regiments of Life Guards were each organized on five troops, a single troop comprising 150 soldiers, divided into three small companies of fifty men. Four troops were assembled together to form two active squadrons, while the remaining troop acted as a regimental depot. In 1799, a sixth troop was added to both regiments in order to form a reserve squadron. The Royal Horse Guards were not part (at least officially) of the Royal Household, and thus at the beginning of the Revolutionary Wars they had an internal establishment of eight troops, which was different from that of the two regiments of Life Guards. In 1812, however, the Life Guards were reorganized on eight troops each. However, each troop of the Life Guards still had only fifty troopers, so their numbers were smaller than those of the Horse Guards. Consequently, in 1809, each regiment of Life Guards comprised 416 officers and men, while the regiment of Horse Guards mustered 654 officers and men. In 1812, the internal establishment of the Horse Guards was expanded to ten troops, but again reduced to eight with demobilization in 1814.

Before the outbreak of the Revolutionary Wars against France, each British 'line' heavy cavalry regiment consisted of six troops that were assembled into three

Trooper of the 1st Dragoon Guards with M1812 uniform.

squadrons, one of which was a depot unit that was always kept in reserve in Britain and was never sent to serve overseas. The depot squadron of each regiment had to provide new recruits with some solid basic training to the two active squadrons in order to replenish the losses suffered during overseas deployments. In 1793, with the war mobilization that followed the outbreak of hostilities with France, the standard establishment of a heavy cavalry regiment was increased from six to nine troops; this organizational change, however, was not immediately adopted by all units, with several regiments continuing to have a variable number of troops for some time. In 1800, the troops in each unit were increased to ten, in order to form four active squadrons and one depot squadron. However, the number of active squadrons was reduced to three in 1811, and thus the number of troops in each regiment was fixed at eight (six active and two at the depot).

The standard regimental staff of the heavy cavalry units comprised the following elements: one colonel, two lieutenant colonels, two majors, six captains, one captain lieutenant, eight lieutenants, nine cornets, one paymaster, one adjutant, one surgeon, two assistant surgeons and one veterinary surgeon. The three guard units of the British cavalry had irregular regimental staffs, whose composition varied greatly during the Napoleonic Wars. By 1815, however, the 1st Life Guards had one colonel, two supernumerary lieutenant colonels, one major, eight captains, eight lieutenants, six cornets, one adjutant, one surgeon, two assistant surgeons and two veterinary surgeons. The 2nd Life Guards had one colonel, two supernumerary lieutenant colonels, one major, eight captains, eight lieutenants, seven cornets, one adjutant, two surgeons, one assistant surgeon and two veterinary surgeons, while the Horse Guards had one colonel, two supernumerary lieutenant colonels, two majors, ten captains, eleven lieutenants, eight cornets, one adjutant, one surgeon, two assistant surgeons and two veterinary surgeons. A standard heavy cavalry troop included one lieutenant colonel, one major, one captain, one quartermaster (sergeant-major since 1809), four sergeants, four corporals, one trumpeter and eighty-five troopers. The troops of the Life Guards and the Horse Guards continued to comprise a quartermaster after 1809, but they did not have sergeants.

Uniforms and equipment

Until 1796, the British heavy cavalry continued to wear its pre-revolutionary uniforms, which comprised black bicorn hat and red tail-coat with open lapels on the front, which were in the distinctive colour of each regiment. In 1796, the lapels started to be worn buttoned up in order to form a single frontal plastron. A year later, in 1797, a new model of tail-coat was introduced. This was single-breasted and did not have lapels on the front, so it was much more comfortable to wear. All regiments had red uniforms, except for the Horse Guards, who were dressed in their distinctive dark blue. In 1812, there was a revolution in the uniforms of the British heavy cavalry, with a new and much more modern dress introduced. This had a black leather helmet and substituted the old-fashioned tail-coat with a single-breasted jacket with short turnbacks. These M1812 uniforms were retained in service until the end of the Napoleonic Wars. The pre-1797 dress was as follows for the Life Guards: black bicorn with yellow external edging, black cockade with yellow lace holder and white-and-red plume; red coat with dark blue collar patches and round cuffs, dark blue frontal lapels, dark blue shoulder straps with yellow piping and fringes; additional

Trooper of the 1st Dragoon Guards with M1812 dress.

stripes of yellow lace on the buttonholes of the collar patches (two), front of the coat (eight), cuffs (one) and sleeves (three); and V-shaped buttonholes on the cuffs and sleeves. White turnbacks, white trousers, black leather tall boots and white leather belt equipment completed their dress. The uniform of the Horse Guards was similar, but it had dark blue as its main colour instead of red: black bicorn with yellow external edging, black cockade with yellow lace holder and white-and-red plume; dark blue coat with red collar patches and round cuffs, red frontal lapels, red shoulder straps with yellow piping and fringes; additional stripes of yellow lace on the buttonholes of the collar patches (two), front of the coat (eight), cuffs (one) and sleeves (three); and V-shaped buttonholes on the cuffs and sleeves. They also had white turnbacks, buff trousers, black leather tall boots and buff leather belt equipment. During 1794 – for a brief period – the Blues wore a white metal cuirass over their uniforms, which was similar to that used by the contemporary French cuirassiers. This was worn together with a buff leather waist belt that had a black leather ammunition pouch on the front. Officers of both the Life Guards and Horse Guards had all the yellow elements listed above in gold, wore a red sash wrapped around the waist, and had their rank indicated by golden epaulettes and contre-epaulettes that were worn on the shoulders instead of the shoulder straps.

The M1797 dress was as follows for the Life Guards: black bicorn with yellow external edging, black cockade with yellow lace holder and white-and-red plume; red coat with dark blue collar and round cuffs, dark blue shoulder straps with yellow piping; additional stripes of yellow lace on the buttonholes of the collar (two), front of the coat (eight in four couples), cuffs (one) and sleeves (three); and V-shaped buttonholes on the cuffs and sleeves. White turnbacks, white trousers, black leather tall boots and white leather belt equipment completed their uniform. The uniform of the Horse Guards was again similar, but with dark blue as the main colour instead of red: black bicorn with yellow external edging, black cockade with yellow lace holder and white-and-red plume; dark blue coat with red collar and round cuffs, red shoulder straps with yellow piping; additional stripes of yellow lace on the buttonholes of the collar (two), front of the coat (eight in four couples), cuffs (one) and sleeves (three); and V-shaped buttonholes on the cuffs and sleeves. They also had white turnbacks, buff trousers, black leather tall boots and buff leather belt equipment.

The Life Guards and Horse Guards adopted new uniforms introduced for the line heavy cavalry in 1812 only during 1813–1814, after their deployment in the Iberian Peninsula. The new dress comprised the following for the Life Guards: black leather helmet with brass frontal plate bearing the royal monogram on the front, brass peak, brass chinscale, brass crest covered with half-black and half-red fur (black at the top, red at the bottom), and white-and-red plume (white at the top, red at the bottom,

Troopers of the 2nd Dragoons (left) and the 3rd Dragoons (right), both with M1812 uniform. Note the massive bearskin of the Scots Greys on the left.

like the previous one worn on the bicorn); red single-breasted jacket with dark blue collar and round cuffs, both piped in yellow, yellow shoulder straps piped in dark blue, yellow piping to the front and bottom edges of the jacket, dark blue turnbacks piped in yellow (these were short and not long as in the previous dress), white trousers, black leather boots and white leather belt equipment. Around the waist, a red-and-yellow sash was worn. This dress was worn on parade, being substituted by a simpler one on campaign which differed in some elements: the collar and cuffs of the jacket did not have yellow piping but additional yellow lace on the buttonholes; the piping to the front and bottom edges of the jacket was not yellow but dark blue; the shoulder straps were dark blue with red piping; and the white trousers were replaced by dark grey ones with red double side-stripe. The Horse Guards replaced their old uniform with bicorn and coat only around 1814, some months after the Life Guards. Their new dress was as follows: black leather helmet with brass frontal plate bearing the royal monogram on the front, brass peak, brass chinscale, brass crest covered with half-dark blue and half-red fur (dark blue at the top, red at the bottom), and white-and-red plume (white at the top, red at the bottom, like the previous one worn on the bicorn); dark blue single-breasted jacket with red collar and round cuffs, both piped in yellow, red shoulder straps piped in yellow, yellow piping to the front and bottom edges of the jacket, red turnbacks piped in yellow (these were short and not long as in the previous dress), buff trousers, black leather boots and buff leather belt equipment. Around the waist, a red-and-yellow sash was worn. This dress was worn on parade, and was replaced by a simpler one on campaign, which again differed in some elements: the collar and cuffs of the jacket did not have yellow piping but there was additional yellow lace on the buttonholes; the piping to the front and bottom edges of the jacket was not yellow but white; the shoulder straps were dark blue with yellow piping; and the buff trousers were replaced by dark grey ones with red double side-stripe. Officers of all three guard regiments, both with parade dress and campaign dress, wore the same uniforms as their men, but with all the yellow elements in gold and with golden shoulder straps showing their rank. The shabraque used by both the Life Guards and Horse Guards was dark blue, with the royal monogram embroidered in gold on the back corner and on the pistols' holsters; it had a golden band on the external edge, with red piping in the centre.

Chapter 2

The Heavy Cavalry

History and organization

At the outbreak of the Revolutionary Wars, the British heavy cavalry consisted of two distinct categories of units: the Dragoon Guards and the Dragoons. While the former were made up of heavy horsemen and the latter of medium horsemen, in practice there was very little difference between them since both were trained and equipped to act as 'shock cavalry', and as such acted differently tactically to the regiments of Light Dragoons (which will be covered in the next chapter).

The Dragoon Guards were first created in 1746, when the organization of the British heavy cavalry underwent a radical reform. The first two heavy cavalry units that received the new denomination of Dragoon Guards were the Queen's Own Regiment of Horse and the Earl of Peterborough's Regiment of Horse, which respectively became the 1st and the 2nd Dragoon Guards. In 1747, a third unit, the Earl of Plymouth's Regiment of Horse, was converted into a regiment of Dragoon Guards. This was followed by another four units in 1788, when the British cavalry was again reorganized; so by 1790, the British Army included a total of seven regiments of Dragoon Guards. Since the days of the Restoration (1660), the English cavalry had been made up of horse regiments and dragoon regiments. Horse regiments were equipped with cuirasses until the late seventeenth century and consisted of proper heavy cavalry, while the dragoon regiments were originally raised as mounted infantry corps that were not tasked with conducting frontal charges. Initially, the dragoons were introduced in European armies from the mid-seventeenth century as chosen units of infantrymen who could use horses to travel long distance or to move on the battlefield, but who dismounted to fight. In practice, they consisted of infantrymen with a higher degree of mobility, which was clear from their personal equipment, since they were armed with long infantry muskets and did not wear the leather boots used by the cavalrymen of the horse regiments. Over time, notably during the early eighteenth century, the dragoons gradually lost their original mounted infantry nature and transformed themselves into normal line cavalry. At the same time, the horse regiments discarded their metal cuirasses and started to use lighter personal equipment. As a result of these changes, the existing tactical differences that distinguished horse regiments from the dragoon units practically

Trooper of the 3rd Dragoons with M1812 dress.

ceased to exist. Neither heavy horsemen nor dragoons now wore cuirasses, and they were now employed to perform the same duties. As a result, in 1746, the British government decided to transform the horse regiments into dragoons in order to cut costs and to eliminate a tactical differentiation that no longer existed in practice. The heavy mounts of the horse regiments had a considerable cost but produced no real advantages during battle, while those in the horse regiments had the privilege of being paid much more than dragoon units.

With the creation of the Dragoon Guards, the British government found a good compromise: the costly horse regiments were abolished, but at the same time their members kept alive the glorious traditions of the British heavy cavalry. The term 'Guards' of their new official denomination underlined that the units of Dragoon Guards were the elite of the British heavy cavalry, marking a formal difference between them and the regular dragoons. The transformation of the horse regiments into Dragoon Guards was very unpopular among the affected units, since it led to drastic reductions in pay. In addition, the new official denomination did not signify the inclusion of the old horse regiments into the Royal Household. In practice, the Dragoon Guards were placed between the Life Guards/Horse Guards and the regular regiments of dragoons. By the outbreak of the Revolutionary Wars, there were six dragoon regiments, so the British Army's heavy cavalry now comprised thirteen regiments (the reduction to thirteen taking place in 1799).

For each regiment of Dragoon Guards, there now follows a short unit history (paying special attention to the actions fought during the Napoleonic era):

1st Dragoon Guards: Raised in 1685, they were originally named the Queen's Own Regiment of Horse in honour of Queen Mary (the consort of James II). With the outbreak of the Glorious Revolution, they joined William of Orange's cause, taking part in the Battle of the Boyne (1690) and the following Battle of Aughrim (1691). Shortly before the birth of the British Army, the 1st Dragoon Guards participated in all the most important battles fought by Marlborough during the War of the Spanish Succession: Blenheim (1704), Ramillies (1706), Oudenarde (1708) and Malplaquet (1709). In 1714, with the arrival of the House of Hanover in Great Britain, they were renamed as the 2nd King's Own Regiment of Horse in honour to the new king, George I. With this new denomination, the regiment took part in the Battle of Dettingen in 1743, during the War of the Austrian Succession. Following the outbreak of the Jacobite Rebellion in Scotland, they were transformed into the 1st Regiment of Dragoon Guards. In 1760, during the Seven Years' War, the corps distinguished itself at the Battle of Corbach and the Battle of Warburg. In 1793, with the outbreak of war with France, the regiment's internal establishment was

Officers of the KGL's 1st Dragoons with M1797 uniform.

augmented from nine to twelve troops, only half of which were sent to continental Europe to fight against the French. After taking part with distinction in the Flanders campaign, the troops of the regiment were reduced to seven (1795). During 1798, one troop was added to the regiment, followed by another two in 1800. During the following ten years, the unit remained on garrison duty in England and Ireland and was expanded back to twelve troops. During 1814, two of the regiment's troops were temporarily disbanded, but they were soon re-raised when Napoleon returned to France after his first exile. Finally, after many years of inactivity, the regiment was sent to Belgium in 1815 and participated with distinction in the British cavalry charges at Waterloo.

2nd Dragoon Guards: Raised in 1685, they were originally called the Earl of Peterborough's Regiment of Horse. With the outbreak of the Glorious Revolution, they joined William of Orange's cause and participated in the Battle of the Boyne (1690) and the Battle of Aughrim (1691). During the War of the Spanish Succession, they were sent to Portugal to fight against the Bourbon forces that operated in the Iberian Peninsula, taking part in the Battle of Almenar (1710). After returning home, the regiment contributed to the suppression of the 1715 Jacobite Uprising. In 1746, following the second Jacobite Uprising that was defeated at the Battle of Culloden, the unit became the 2nd Regiment of Dragoon Guards. In 1760, during the Seven Years' War, the corps distinguished itself at the Battle of Corbach and the Battle of Warburg, then fought brilliantly at the Battle of Wilhelmsthal (1762). In 1793, with the outbreak of war with France, the regiment's internal establishment was strengthened from nine to twelve troops, ten of which were sent to continental Europe to fight against the French. After taking part with distinction in the Flanders campaign, the regiment was reduced to eight troops (1795). In 1799, two troops were added to the regiment, but were disbanded in 1802 during the reorganization of the British Army that followed the signing of the Peace of Amiens. In 1806, the number of troops was increased again to ten. Three years later, six troops from the regiment participated in the unsuccessful Walcheren campaign in the Netherlands. In 1813, eight of the regiment's ten troops were made ready for service in the Iberian Peninsula, but they did not embark. During 1814, two of the regiment's troops were temporarily disbanded, but were quickly re-raised when Napoleon returned to France from Elba. Although the regiment was sent to Belgium, it did not arrive in time to fight at Waterloo. It remained on the continent as part of the British Army of Occupation.

3rd Dragoon Guards: Raised in 1685, they were originally known as the Earl of Plymouth's Regiment of Horse. After the Glorious Revolution, the regiment served with distinction during the War of the Spanish Succession, participating in the following battles: Schellenberg (1704), Blenheim (1704), Ramillies (1706), Oudenarde (1708) and Malplaquet (1709). In 1747, the regiment was transformed into the 3rd Regiment of Dragoon Guards. After taking part in the Flanders campaign against Revolutionary France, the unit remained on garrison duty in England and Ireland until being dispatched to the Iberian Peninsula in 1809. The 3rd Regiment of Dragoon Guards served in Spain until 1813, seeing action at Talavera (1809), Albuhera (1811) and Vittoria (1813). Of the ten troops that made up the unit, eight fought in the Iberian Peninsula and two remained in Great Britain. In 1814, after participating in the invasion of southern France, the internal establishment of the regiment was reduced to eight troops. The unit did not take part in the Battle of Waterloo, but sent six of its troops to France to act as part of the British Army of Occupation.

4th Dragoon Guards: Raised in 1685, they were originally named the Earl of Arran's Regiment of Horse. With the outbreak of the Glorious Revolution, they joined William of Orange's cause, participating in the Battle of the Boyne (1690) and to various subsequent actions that took place in Ireland. In 1746, the unit was transferred to the Irish establishment of the British Army, of which it remained part until being transferred back to the English establishment in 1788. In that same year, it became the 4th Regiment of Dragoon Guards (Royal Irish). At the beginning of the Revolutionary Wars, the number of troops in the unit was expanded to nine. In 1798, the regiment contributed to the crushing of the Irish Rebellion (which was supported by France). In 1800, the regiment was expanded to ten troops, but this organizational change was short-lived since the unit was reduced to just eight troops in 1802. After spending several years in England, garrisoning the countryside and suppressing local riots, the 4th Dragoon Guards were again expanded to ten troops, with six being sent to Portugal (1811). During 1812, the regiment fought at Ciudad Rodrigo and Badajoz. After returning home in March 1813, the 4th Dragoon Guards did not take part in any other combat until the end of the Napoleonic Wars.

5th Dragoon Guards: Raised in 1686, they were originally known as the Earl of Shrewsbury's Regiment of Horse. With the outbreak of the Glorious Revolution, they joined William of Orange's cause and fought at the Battle of the Boyne (1690) and the First Siege of Limerick (1690). During the War of the Spanish Succession, the regiment took part in the Battle of Blenheim (1704), as well as those at Ramillies (1706) and Malplaquet (1708). During the following eighty years, the regiment remained on garrison duty in Ireland, without seeing action in continental Europe. In 1788, the corps became the new 5th Regiment of Dragoon Guards, then five years later was sent to Flanders where it participated in the campaign against Revolutionary France. With its internal establishment of ten troops, the regiment was among the British units that crushed the Irish Rebellion of 1798. For a short period, from 1802–1803, the regiment's number of troops was reduced from ten to eight. In 1811, six of the now ten troops were sent to Portugal, serving with distinction at the Battle of Salamanca the following year. The 5th Dragoon Guards continued to serve in the Iberian Peninsula during 1813, fighting at Vittoria. In 1814, the regiment followed

Troopers of the KGL's 1st Dragoons (left) and the KGL's 2nd Dragoons (right), both with M1797 dress.

Wellington in his invasion of southern France and took part in the Battle of Toulouse. Reduced to just eight troops, the unit returned to Britain and did not take part in the Belgian campaign of 1815.

6th Dragoon Guards: Raised in 1686, they were originally known as Lord Lumley's Regiment of Horse. During the Glorious Revolution, they joined William of Orange's cause and went to Ireland to fight against the Jacobite forces. They were later sent to continental Europe and participated in the War of the Grand Alliance, which was fought between France and a large multinational coalition of states that included England. In 1692, the unit was renamed as the King's Regiment of Carabineers, under which denomination it took part in the War of the Spanish Succession and fought at Blenheim (1704) and Ramillies (1706). In 1745, it was part of the British forces that crushed the Jacobite Uprising. Some years later, it was transferred to the Irish establishment of the British Army, remaining so until 1788, when it was transferred back to the English establishment and became the 6th Regiment of Dragoon Guards. In 1793, it was sent to continental Europe and saw action against the French in Flanders, where it fought with distinction. From 1796–1807, the regiment was part of the British garrison in Ireland, taking part in the bloody repression of the 1798 Irish Rebellion. In 1806, a detachment of 400 officers and men from the 6th Dragoon Guards was sent to South America and took part in the ill-fated British expedition against Buenos Aires (Argentina was at the time still a colony of Spain, and the latter was an ally of Napoleon). This campaign and a similar one in 1807 both proved to be complete failures. After this overseas mission, the regiments remained on garrison duty in England and Ireland until the end of the Napoleonic Wars, not taking part in any major engagement against the French.

7th Dragoon Guards: Raised in 1688, they were originally named Lord Cavendish's Regiment of Horse. Despite being organized to provide a mounted escort for Princess Anne, the younger daughter of James II, the unit soon joined William of Orange when he landed in England. During the Williamite Wars that were fought in Ireland between the new English monarch and the Jacobite rebels, the regiment took part in the Battle of the Boyne (1690) before being sent to continental Europe. Here, it participated in the War of the Grand Alliance and operated against the French forces of Louis XIV. The corps returned to continental Europe with the outbreak of the War of the Spanish Succession War, fighting with distinction at Blenheim (1704), Elixheim (1705), Ramillies (1706) and Malplaquet (1709). After the end of hostilities, the unit spent several years in Ireland where it acted as a garrison corps. In 1742, the regiment served in Flanders after the outbreak of the War of the Austrian Succession, seeing action at the Battle of Dettingen in 1743 and the Battle of Fontenoy in 1745. After another period of garrison duty in Ireland, the unit was sent back to continental Europe to fight in the Seven Years' War, being noted for its efforts at the Battle of Warburg in 1760. In 1788, the unit was transformed into the 7th Regiment of Dragoon Guards, and during the following years it remained on garrison duty in England and Ireland. In 1798, it helped crush the Irish Rebellion. The regiment never served overseas during the Napoleonic Wars.

Analyzing the regimental histories of the seven regiments of Dragoon Guards, it is possible to find several common elements. First of all, these units were all organized during the reign of James II, most of them to help suppress the Monmouth Rebellion that broke out in 1685. Until their transformation into Dragoon Guards corps, the regiments participated in all the major battles fought by Britain on the continent during the eighteenth century (in the War of the Spanish Succession, War of the Austrian Succession and Seven Years' War). With their transformation into Dragoon Guards corps, their employment changed dramatically: after 1788, the regiments were sent to serve overseas only on very rare occasions, and thus spent most of their regimental life as garrison troops in Britain. The Dragoon Guards were deployed in Ireland, where they were tasked with patrolling the countryside and preventing the outbreak of local uprisings. Apparently, the British government considered the Dragoon Guards as a sort of strategic reserve, preferring to keep them on garrison duty at home. These horsemen had the necessary training and expertise to act like the contemporary French Gendarmerie (reorganized as a military police corps after the outbreak of the French Revolution). This trend was confirmed during the Napoleonic Wars, since the Dragoon Guards seldom fought overseas.

As we will see from their regimental histories below, the units of dragoons were employed much more frequently in combat than the Dragoon Guards (especially during the Napoleonic Wars):

1st Dragoons: This regiment, the oldest dragoon unit of the British Army, was organized in 1661 (shortly after the Restoration of Charles II) from veterans of the disbanded Parliamentary Army. Initially, it consisted of just one troop, but it was later expanded to four before being sent to serve in Tangier. Located on the coastline of Morocco, the city of Tangier was an English colony from 1661–1684, and thus needed to have a proper garrison in order to be defended from attacks by England's colonial rivals. The four troops of dragoons, collectively known as the Tangier Horse, served in Morocco until 1678, and were then sent to Scotland in order to police the local Covenanters (a Presbyterian movement that caused some political troubles to the central government). In 1680, the unit was disbanded and its men were sent back to Tangiers as reinforcements for the local garrison. However, they returned to England in 1683 and were reorganized as an independent regiment of dragoons. This was expanded to six troops and assumed the new denomination of The Royal Regiment of Dragoons. Like most of the English military units, after the outbreak of the Glorious Revolution they became part of the Williamite army and as such participated in the Battle of the Boyne and the First Siege of Limerick (both fought in 1690). During the War of the Austrian Succession, the regiment participated in the Battle of Dettingen (1743) and the Battle of Fontenoy (1745), assuming the denomination of the 1st Royal Regiment of Dragoons in 1751. The unit took part

Trooper of the KGL's 1st Dragoons with M1797 uniform.

Trooper of the heavy cavalry with the undress uniform worn inside barracks.

in the Seven Years' War and fought with note at the Battle of Warburg in 1760. With the outbreak of hostilities with Revolutionary France, the corps sent four of its ten troops to Flanders. Between 1796 and 1801, the regiment remained on garrison duty along the coast of southern England, where it mostly performed anti-smuggler duties. For a brief period, from 1802–1803, its internal establishment was reduced from ten to eight troops. In January 1807, the unit was transferred to Ireland, where it remained until 1809. During summer of 1809, eight troops from the regiment were sent to the Iberian Peninsula. Here they remained until 1813, taking part in several minor combat actions and being temporarily reduced to six troops in 1811. After joining Wellington's invasion of southern France in 1814, the 1st Dragoons were permanently reduced to six troops. In 1815, the regiment became part of the famous Union Brigade and was sent to continental Europe to fight against Napoleon in the Belgian campaign. Together with the 2nd and 6th Dragoons that made up with it the Union Brigade, the 1st Dragoons participated in the famous cavalry charge that stabilized the British front during the Battle of Waterloo. The troopers of the 1st Dragoons distinguished themselves during the fighting, capturing the Imperial Eagle of a French line infantry regiment. The nickname 'Union Brigade' derived from the fact that it was made up of regiments from different areas of the United Kingdom: the 1st Dragoons from England, the 2nd Dragoons from Scotland and the 6th Dragoons from Ireland.

2nd Dragoons: This regiment was originally raised in 1678 as three independent troops of dragoons that were part of the Scots Army, not of the English Army. At that time, Scotland still had an independent army that was mostly used to perform internal police duties. In 1681, another three troops of dragoons were raised, being assembled together with the existing ones in order to form a new unit that received the name of the Royal Regiment of Scots Dragoons. During this early phase of its history, the unit was already mounted on grey horses and thus later received its famous nickname of the Scots Greys. With the outbreak of the Glorious Revolution, like the rest of the Scots Army, the Royal Regiment of Scots Dragoons sided with William of Orange and helped him crush the revolt of the Scottish Jacobites. During the War of the Spanish Succession, still as part of the Scots Army, the unit fought under Marlborough with great distinction. At that time, the dragoons were still mostly employed as mounted infantrymen, and as such they participated to the following battles: Schellenberg (1704), Blenheim (1704), Elixheim (1705), Ramillies (1706), Oudenarde (1708) and Malplaquet (1709). After assuming the new denomination of the Royal North British Dragoons, the regiment was – like the rest of the Scots Army – absorbed into the new British Army. After returning to their homeland, the Scots Greys remained loyal to the House of Hanover upon the outbreak of the Jacobite Rising of 1715. The Scottish dragoons fought with great determination against the rebels, and were one of the key factors behind the final victory of the British forces. After the end of the rising in 1719, the regiment remained for more than two decades on garrison duty in Scotland and continued to perform the main task for which it had been created: policing Scotland and preventing the outbreak of risings among the Highland clans. In 1742, two years after the beginning of the War of the Austrian Succession, the Scots Greys were sent to Flanders to fight against the French. Like several other British cavalry units, the regiment fought at Dettingen in 1743 and Fontenoy in 1745; during the latter clash, the Scots Greys covered the retreat of the defeated British infantry. When the second Jacobite Rising of 1745 began, the corps was not transferred to Scotland, and thus remained in Flanders until the end of the War of the Austrian Succession in 1748. During 1755, for a very short period, a single company of light cavalry was added to the establishment of the regiment, but this was soon detached from it and became an independent corps. With the outbreak of the Seven Years' War, the Scots Greys were sent to Germany, where they operated together with the forces of Hanover. In 1759, the regiment fought at Bergen and Minden, but had little opportunity to show its valour. During the following year, however, the Scots Greys conducted a brilliant frontal charge which proved decisive at the Battle of Warburg. Before the end of the conflict, in 1762, the Scottish regiment took part in the Battle of Wilhelmsthal, during which it attacked already-routed French troops (capturing many prisoners and even part of the French baggage train). During the long period from 1764–1793, the Scots Greys remained in Britain, performing garrison duties and not taking part in any combat action. In 1768, they replaced their distinctive mitre-style grenadier caps with the tall bearskins that they later famously wore at the Battle of Waterloo. During this same period, one troop of Light Dragoons was attached to each troop of the regiment, but this organizational change lasted for just a few years; in 1779, all the detachments of Light Dragoons were assembled together to form an independent unit of light cavalry.

Before the outbreak of hostilities with Revolutionary France, the Scots Greys were organized on five troops, but when the war began, these were rapidly increased to nine. During 1793 and 1794, the Scots Greys operated with the British expeditionary force that was deployed in Flanders, helping obtain a remarkable victory over the French at the Battle of Tournai. During this clash, the Scottish regiment managed to break a defensive formation of the enemy infantry, which was deployed in squares. In 1795, the four troops of the Scots Greys that had served in continental Europe returned home, where the whole regiment was reduced to eight troops. During the following

Trumpeter of the 17th Light Dragoons with pre-1784 dress; with the latter, trumpeters wore a standard bicorn instead of the leather helmet used by troopers. Note the rich livery that was distinctive of musicians.

years, despite the fact that Britain was fighting against Napoleon around the globe, the Scottish unit was never sent to serve overseas. When Bonaparte returned to France in 1815, however, the Scots Greys were mobilized and their internal establishment was increased to ten troops. Six of the troops were sent to Belgium as part of the famous Union Brigade, a large heavy cavalry formation that comprised three regiments of dragoons. At Waterloo, the Scots Greys were deployed in the third line of Wellington's army, on the left flank. When Napoleon ordered a general advance of his infantry against the centre of the British forces, the Household Brigade and the Union Brigade received the order to counter-attack in order to stabilize the British line. The Scots Greys were intended to remain back during the charge and act as a reserve in case the attack should fail. Seeing that the British infantry were about to be routed, the commander of the regiment decided to charge the attacking French. The charge of the regiment, which advanced at the cry of 'Scotland forever!', devastated the French infantry, who were moving in open order and did not have time to form defensive squares. Consequently, the Scots Greys could charge very deeply into their ranks and kill many Frenchmen. During the furious assault, the Scottish soldiers even managed to capture the Imperial Eagle of an enemy infantry regiment. After routing the French troops that were attacking the British lines, the regiment, instead of re-forming, continued its advance and found itself in front of the main French line. By now their horses were blown and their formation was disorganized, and they were counter-charged by French cuirassiers and lancers. The Union Brigade suffered very heavy losses during this phase of the battle, and even its commander, William Ponsonby, was killed. Under heavy French artillery fire, and with enemy cavalry in close pursuit, the exhausted British cavalrymen returned to their lines after suffering severe casualties. Nevertheless, their dramatic frontal charge had saved Wellington's line from collapse and helped determine the ultimate outcome of the battle.

3rd Dragoons: Raised in 1685 as the Queen's Regiment of Dragoons, it originally consisted of six troops and soon joined William of Orange when he landed in England to launch the Glorious Revolution. During 1690 and 1691, the unit fought against the Jacobites in Ireland, before being sent to continental Europe in order to participate in the War of the Grand Alliance. At the beginning of the new century, the regiment was sent to serve overseas with the outbreak of the War of the Spanish Succession, during which the corps was deployed in the Iberian Peninsula and fought at the bloody Battle of Almansa. In 1715, after returning home, it joined the British forces that were tasked with suppressing the Jacobite Uprising. During the following decades, the regiment remained on garrison duty in southern England, where it was mostly employed to combat smuggling. During the War of the Austrian Succession, the unit was sent to continental Europe, where it took part in the Battle of Dettingen (1743) and the Battle of Fontenoy (1745). With the outbreak of the second Jacobite Uprising, the corps was rapidly sent back home and participated in the decisive Battle of Culloden that saw the defeat of the Jacobites. Until the outbreak of the Napoleonic Wars, the regiment did not see much further action except for a few minor clashes with the French during the Seven Years' War. The 3rd Dragoons did not take part in the Flanders campaign of 1793–1795. In 1809, however, they were selected to be part of the British expeditionary force that landed in Walcheren (Netherlands), but many of them, like the rest of the British soldiers involved, caught the terrible disease known as 'Walcheren Fever' and died without seeing action against the French. In 1810, the regiment was on garrison duty in England and suppressed various local protests, before being sent to Portugal during the following year. In 1812, the 3rd Dragoons took part in the sieges of Ciudad Rodrigo and Badajoz, and successfully charged the French at the Battle of Salamanca. In 1813, the regiment served under Wellington at the decisive Battle of Vittoria, and it took part in the British invasion of southern France in 1814, fighting at the Battle of Toulouse. After years of distinguished service in the Iberian Peninsula, the 3rd Dragoons returned home and was not involved in the Belgian campaign of 1815. In 1818, the unit was transformed into a regiment of Light Dragoons.

4th Dragoons: Raised in 1685 as Princess Anne of Denmark's Regiment of Dragoons, this regiment joined William of Orange soon after the start of the Glorious Revolution. It was sent to Scotland, where it fought against the local Jacobites, and later served in continental Europe during the War of the Grand Alliance (seeing action on several occasions in Flanders). During the War of the Spanish Succession, it was sent to the Iberian Peninsula and fought with determination at the bloody Battle of Almansa (1707). With the outbreak of the 1715 Jacobite Uprising, it was employed against the Scottish insurgents and took part in the Battle of Sheriffmuir. After many years spent on garrison duty in Britain, the unit returned to continental Europe with the outbreak of the War of the Austrian Succession. During this conflict, it fought at the Battle of Dettingen (1743) and the Battle of Lauffeld (1747). During the American Revolution, the 4th Dragoons remained in Britain and took part in the suppression of the Gordon Riots, which took place in London in 1780. In 1793, they were not sent to Flanders to fight against the French, remaining on garrison duty in Britain until 1809. They were then sent to the Iberian Peninsula, where they fought at the battles of Talavera (1809) and Albuera (1811). In 1812, the regiment was at Salamanca, and in 1813 it fought at Vittoria, on both occasions performing with great distinction. The regiment took part in the British invasion of southern

Troopers of the 10th Light Dragoons with M1784 uniform.

France (1814) before returning home and being reduced from ten to eight troops. It was not involved in the Belgian campaign of 1815, and in 1818 it was transformed into a regiment of Light Dragoons.

5th Dragoons: Raised in 1689 as part of William of Orange's new English Army during the Glorious Revolution, they originally had the official denomination of Colonel Wynn's Regiment of Dragoons. In 1690, the regiment participated in the Williamite Wars in Ireland, fighting at the Battle of the Boyne and the Battle of Aughrim (both fought in 1690). In 1704, the unit was renamed the Royal Dragoons of Ireland and later sent to continental Europe to fight in the War of the Spanish Succession. During the latter conflict it participated in the engagements at Blenheim (1704), Ramillies (1706), Oudenarde (1708) and Malplaquet (1709). During the following decades, the regiment remained on garrison duty in Ireland, where it was mostly tasked with patrolling the countryside and preventing the outbreak of local revolts. With the outbreak of the Irish Rebellion in 1798, the 5th Dragoons played a crucial role in suppressing the activities of the insurgents and took part in the Battle of Enniscorthy. Before and after the Irish Rebellion, the regiment was dispersed in many small detachments across Ireland. This lack of regimental unity had extremely negative consequences for the morale of the corps, whose members were accused of treachery and sedition in 1799. After an official investigation, the regiment was disbanded in late 1799 and was erased from the records of the British Army.

6th Dragoons: Raised in 1689 for William of Orange's new English Army at the time of the Glorious Revolution, the unit was originally called Richard Cunningham's Regiment of Dragoons. It soon received the famous nickname of the 'Inniskilling Dragoons' since it was quartered in Inniskilling Castle (in northern Ireland). In 1690, the regiment fought at the decisive Battle of the Boyne and later remained in Ireland for some time. When the Jacobite Rising of 1715 began, it was transferred to Scotland, where it fought against the Jacobites at the Battle of Sheriffmuir. With the outbreak of the War of the Austrian Secession, the regiment was transferred to continental Europe, where it participated in the following battles: Dettingen (1743), Fontenoy (1745), Rocoux (1746) and Lauffeld (1747). During the Seven Years' War, the corps was sent to fight against France, featuring in the engagements at Minden and Wetter (both in 1759). Between 1793 and 1795, the 6th Dragoons were deployed in Flanders and fought in several actions against the French. From 1802–1803, for just a few months, the internal establishment of the regiment was reduced from ten to eight troops. The unit remained on garrison duty in Britain until 1815, spending most of the time in Ireland and being reduced to nine troops in 1814. When Napoleon returned from exile to France, six troops of the 6th Dragoons were sent to Belgium, where they took part in the Battle of Waterloo as part of the Union Brigade. Like the Scots Greys, the members of the regiment distinguished themselves during the cavalry charge that helped stabilize the British front.

As is clear from these potted regimental histories, the dragoons of the British Army played an important role during the Napoleonic Wars, but their military contribution was more important from a qualitative point of view than from a quantitative one. It should be noted that after the disbandment of the 5th Dragoons, the British Army could deploy a total of only 12 heavy cavalry regiments; of these, seven were Guard Dragoons and were employed overseas only on rare occasions. The heavy cavalry of the British Army was always considered as a strategic reserve, being kept on garrison duties at home whenever possible. Its units were never sent to serve in the colonies, for example in the Thirteen Colonies of North America when the American Revolution began. Furthermore, they participated in the continental wars fought by Britain in Europe only when absolutely necessary. As we will see in the next chapter, the regiments of Light Dragoons were sent to serve overseas much more frequently and were much more numerous than those of the heavy cavalry during the Napoleonic period. From an organizational point of view, it is important to remember that the regiments of Light Dragoons were numbered in progressive order after the six of dragoons, so their first unit was the 7th Regiment of Light Dragoons.

The heavy cavalry regiments of the British Army were structured on troops, two of which made up a squadron. Squadrons were known by letters, with troops known by numbers. Before the outbreak of the Revolutionary Wars against France, each British heavy cavalry regiment consisted of six troops that were assembled into three squadrons; of the latter, one was a depot unit that was kept in reserve in Britain and was never sent to serve overseas. The depot squadron of each regiment had to provide new recruits with some solid basic training for the two active squadrons in order to replenish the losses suffered by them during overseas deployments. In 1793, with the war mobilization that followed the outbreak of hostilities with France, the standard establishment of a heavy cavalry regiment was increased from six to nine troops (ten in some cases, like for the 1st Dragoon Guards or the 1st Dragoons). However, this organizational change was not immediately adopted by all units, and thus several regiments continued to have a variable number of troops for some time. In 1800, the troops in each unit were increased to ten in order to form four active squadrons and one depot squadron. In 1811, however, the number of active squadrons was reduced to three, so the total of troops in each regiment was fixed at eight (six active and two depot). Again, this organizational change was not adopted by all units straight away.

The regimental staff of the heavy cavalry units comprised the following elements: one colonel, two lieutenant colonels, two majors, six captains, one captain lieutenant, eight lieutenants, nine cornets, one paymaster, one adjutant, one surgeon, two assistant surgeons and one veterinary surgeon. Each troop included the following: one lieutenant colonel, one major, one captain, one quartermaster, four sergeants, four corporals, one trumpeter and eighty-five troopers. In June 1809, the quartermaster of each troop was transformed into a sergeant major, and a lieutenant quartermaster was added to the staff of each regiment. During 1810, the internal composition of a heavy cavalry unit's regimental staff was modified and now comprised one colonel, one lieutenant colonel, one major, one adjutant, one lieutenant quartermaster, one paymaster, one surgeon, two assistant surgeons, one veterinary surgeon and one regimental sergeant major. The new composition of a single troop was now one captain, one lieutenant, one cornet, one troop sergeant major, three sergeants, four corporals, one trumpeter, one farrier and sixty-three troopers. By 1809, the average numerical consistency of each heavy cavalry regiment was 905 officers and men, the only exception to this rule being the 1st Dragoons, who had 1,083 officers and men (since it still comprised an additional troop).

Trooper of the 7th Light Dragoons with M1796 dress.

Uniforms and equipment

Until 1796, the British heavy cavalry continued to wear its pre-revolutionary uniforms, which comprised black bicorn hat and red tail-coat, the latter with open lapels on the front which were in the distinctive colour of each regiment. In 1796, the lapels started to be worn buttoned-up in order to form a single frontal plastron. The following year, a new model of tail-coat was introduced. This was single-breasted and did not have lapels on the front, and consequently was much more comfortable to wear. There was a major change in the uniforms of the British heavy cavalry in 1812, with the introduction of a new and much modern dress. This had a black leather helmet as headgear and substituted the old-fashioned tail-coat with a single-breasted jacket that had short turnbacks. The M1812 uniforms were retained in service until the end of the Napoleonic Wars. The pre-1797 dress was as follows: black bicorn with white-and-red plume and black cockade having yellow lace holder; red coat with collar and round cuffs in regimental colour, frontal lapels in regimental colour, and additional stripes of yellow lace on the buttonholes of the collar (one), front of the coat (eight

Troopers of the 7th Light Dragoons with M1796 uniform.

in four couples), cuffs (one) and sleeves (three); and the buttonholes on the cuffs and sleeves were V-shaped. They also had white turnbacks, white trousers, black leather tall boots and white leather belt equipment. Officers had all the yellow elements listed above in gold, and wore a red sash wrapped around the waist. In addition, their rank was shown by golden epaulettes and contre-epaulettes that were worn on the shoulders. The regimental colours, which did not change during the period under consideration, were as follows:

- 1st Dragoon Guards: dark blue
- 2nd Dragoon Guards: black
- 3rd Dragoon Guards: white
- 4th Dragoon Guards: medium blue
- 5th Dragoon Guards: light green
- 6th Dragoon Guards: white
- 7th Dragoon Guards: black
- 1st Dragoons: dark blue
- 2nd Dragoons: dark blue
- 3rd Dragoons: dark blue
- 4th Dragoons: dark green
- 5th Dragoons: dark blue
- 6th Dragoons: yellow

The new M1797 dress comprised the following elements: black bicorn with black cockade having yellow lace holder and with white-and-red plume; red coat with collar and round cuffs in regimental colour, shoulder straps in regimental colour with white or yellow piping, red shoulder wings piped in white or yellow; and additional stripes of white or yellow lace on the buttonholes of the collar (two), front of the coat (ten in five couples), cuffs (one) and sleeves (one). They also had turnbacks in regimental colour, white trousers, black leather tall boots and white leather belt equipment. Officers had all the white/yellow elements listed above in gold and wore a red sash wrapped around the waist, while the shoulder straps and shoulder wings of their uniforms were covered with golden scales. The Scots Greys were the only regiment that did not have the bicorn as headgear; they wore a black bearskin that was retained in service after the introduction of the new M1812 dress. This had a brass frontal plate reproducing the British coat-of-arms, a black leather peak, white plume, brass chinscale and decorative white cord with two tassels of the same colour. In addition, on the back it was ornamented with a red circle, inside which a white 'Horse of Hanover' was embroidered. On campaign, the plume of the bearskin was removed and the whole headgear was protected by a cover made of oilskin. The

Trooper of the 7th Light Dragoons with M1807 hussar dress.

piping colour of the various units could be white or yellow and helped to distinguish the corps having the same regimental colour, according to the following scheme:

- 1st Dragoon Guards: yellow
- 2nd Dragoon Guards: white
- 3rd Dragoon Guards: yellow
- 4th Dragoon Guards: white
- 5th Dragoon Guards: yellow
- 6th Dragoon Guards: white
- 7th Dragoon Guards: yellow
- 1st Dragoons: yellow
- 2nd Dragoons: white
- 3rd Dragoons: yellow
- 4th Dragoons: white
- 5th Dragoons: white
- 6th Dragoons: white

The new M1812 uniform comprised the following elements: black leather helmet with brass frontal plate bearing the royal monogram on the front, black leather peak, brass chinscale and brass crest covered with a black mane and having a black tuft on the front; red single-breasted jacket with collar and pointed cuffs in regimental colour having white or yellow piping, shoulder straps in regimental colour having white or yellow piping, white or yellow piping to the front and bottom edges of the jacket, turnbacks in regimental colour with white or yellow piping (these were short and not long as in the previous dress), white trousers, black leather boots and white leather belt equipment. A sash was worn around the waist, which was in the regimental colour and in the piping colour (white or yellow). On campaign, the white trousers were replaced by dark grey ones with red piping and brown leather reinforcements inside. Officers of all the regiments, both with parade and campaign dress, wore the same uniforms as their men, but with all the white/yellow elements in gold. The shabraque of most regiments was dark blue, with the royal monogram embroidered in the piping colour of each unit on the back corner; on the external edge it had a band in the piping colour of each unit, with dark blue piping in the centre. Some regiments had the shabraque in regimental colour rather than dark blue. Over the shabraque, a protective black or white sheepskin was worn on most occasions. Until 1812, trumpeters were dressed with the standard uniform of their regiment but with reversed colours; from then on, they received the same dress as the ordinary troopers but were easily distinguishable on the battlefield since the mane and tuft of their helmets were red instead of black. In addition, they had decorated shoulder wings.

Chapter 3

The Light Cavalry

History and organization

During the first four decades of the eighteenth century, the heavy cavalry was the most important component of European mounted troops, making up the bulk of the cavalry forces mobilized by the various nations and having acquired a certain tactical supremacy on the battlefield. Highly trained and well-disciplined, the heavy cavalry consisted of horsemen armed with long, straight-bladed swords and mounted on massive horses, which were able to charge and manoeuvre in perfect order by maintaining 'knee-to-knee' close formations. They were mostly employed to conduct frontal charges and to cover the retreat of the line infantry when it was routed by the enemy. However, from the time of the Thirty Years' War, cavalry had started to perform a series of auxiliary roles for the infantry and was rarely used in an autonomous way. At the beginning of the eighteenth century, the tactics and formations of the line infantry were extremely static: while moving on the battlefield, they advanced in columns, deploying into long lines when stopping to open fire upon the enemy. After rolling volleys of musketry were exchanged between two opposing infantry formations, a clash could continue in two different ways: on most occasions, one of the two lines was shattered by the enemy fire and thus decided to retreat (at this point it was usually charged by the enemy cavalry); but it was sometimes necessary to fight 'hand-to-hand' with bayonets to determine the outcome of the confrontation. Keeping order in the formations and delivering a regular fire were the key factors behind victory. Consequently, training was absolutely decisive to transforming line infantry into an effective tactical tool. Generally speaking, battles were extremely static, since maintaining perfect order in the formations obliged both the line infantry and heavy cavalry to move very slowly. The transition from the column formation to the line was extremely delicate, since it exposed the fusiliers to the sudden charges of cavalry. When confronting mounted troops, line infantry usually adopted a standard defensive formation known as the 'square': this was another kind of close order, long-since created to stop enemy attacks by using the bayonets as 'pikes' against mounted troops.

These formations and tactics were determined by the performance of the muskets that were used during the eighteenth century. These were flintlock weapons, for

From the left, troopers of the 15th Light Dragoons, 7th Light Dragoons and 10th Light Dragoons. They are all wearing M1807 uniform.

which the loading operation was quite complicated. This meant that only one or two bullets were shot in a minute, even by a line infantryman with good training. In addition, the flintlock muskets of this period were all smoothbores and thus were extremely inaccurate. When a bullet was fired, it left the weapon without any precise direction since there were no grooves inside the barrel that could 'guide' it. A flintlock musket was of use only when fired some 100–200 metres from the target, so the line infantry formations had to come very close together during a battle in order to use their weapons with some degree of effectiveness. The muskets of this age were also extremely heavy, which greatly limited the mobility of the foot soldiers; when moving on broken terrain, for example that covered with rocks or trees, it was practically impossible for them to keep their close formations in order. All the main tactical formations had been created for employment on an 'ideal' battlefield, consisting of a large plain where the opposing infantry and cavalry could move without encountering obstacles. Due to the weapons' technical limitations, heavy cavalry units made only limited use of firearms. A couple of flintlock pistols were generally carried by each horseman, but these could be fired only from a short distance and thus were of little use. Dragoons, who were by now no longer mounted infantrymen, also carried flintlock carbines, but these were generally used only when they dismounted to fight on foot. In the military system of the early eighteenth century, soldiers were not required to think and act in an autonomous way: they only had to move like clockwork toys in order to put in practice the orders they received. There was no space for initiative, and each infraction of discipline was immediately punished with very harsh methods.

The manoeuvres required on the battlefield were repeated day after day during training sessions, under the incessant beat of drums. A perfect example of the kind of war that was fought in the eighteenth century was represented by the Prussian Army of Frederick the Great, which perfected close line infantry and heavy cavalry tactics and was greatly admired by all the officer corps of Europe. His soldiers were the best of the age and their methods of training were copied by all other armies, whether they be enemies or allies. During the War of the Austrian Succession (1740–1748) and the Seven Years' War (1756–1763), however, several episodes showed that the Prussian heavy cavalry were not as perfect as they may seem. It became apparent that they could experience serious problems while operating on broken terrain and when fighting against enemy units that employed hit-and-run guerrilla tactics.

In particular, the Prussians struggled against the efficient light troops deployed by the Austrian Empire, which consisted of semi-regular light cavalrymen recruited from the inhabitants of the Balkans. The light cavalry of the Austrian Army, commonly known as hussars, had been fighting for decades against the Ottoman Turks on the southern frontier of the Austrian Empire. The Austrians and Turks lived in a state of

Trooper of the 8th Light Dragoons with M1812 dress.

endless conflict, during which both sides usually launched rapid incursions into the territory of their enemy only to raid and pillage as much as possible. Gradually, the Austrian soldiers stationed along the frontier had learned to fight like their enemies, thereby becoming expert in the art of skirmishing and scouting. Their usual area of operations was covered by mountains and woods, where each soldier had to move singly and not in close formation. These fighters were the direct heirs of a glorious military tradition which had originated in Hungary during the late Renaissance: the hussars were the Hungarian national cavalry, like the uhlans (lancers) were for the Polish. Most of the light horsemen from Hungary were farmers during their civilian life and lived on the Balkan frontier as military settlers. As a result, their innovative tactics derived from direct combat experience and were based on the principle of open formation. According to this, each cavalryman advanced in an independent way but always kept contact with the other members of his unit. Consequently, he could cover his advance behind obstacles of the terrain (like a tree, for example) and fire upon the enemy from a favourable position. With such tactics, firearms were also important for cavalry and started to play a prominent role. During the War of the Austrian Succession, the Hungarian light cavalry of the Austrian Army caused serious trouble and losses to Frederick the Great's heavy mounted troops on several occasions. Initially, they were considered as simple 'murderers' by the most traditionalist of their enemies, but over time it became apparent that they could play a very important role on the battlefield.

The other great powers of Europe, differently from Austria, could not count on a militarized border from where expert light mounted fighters could be recruited, so they started to create their own light cavalry corps by recruiting Hungarian mercenaries or prisoners of war. This was the case with France and several other European nations, where hussar units proliferated during the middle of the eighteenth century. The new light horsemen of the European armies adopted the same uniforms and weapons as the Hungarian hussars, but various local variations soon started to appear. In some countries, such as Britain, the new light cavalry assumed some distinctive features from the beginning and was quite different from that of Austria or France. The general expansion of the light cavalry units continued well after the end of the War of the Austrian Succession, since the combat experiences of the following Seven Years' War did nothing but confirm the tactical importance of the new light corps. A new form of warfare was born: the *petite guerre* or 'little war', which was based on low-intensity combat and hit-and-run tactics. The British Army was greatly affected by this light cavalry revolution that took place in the eighteenth century, with its cavalry completely reorganized and modernized during the crucial years that saw the end of the War of the Austrian Succession and the outbreak of the second Jacobite Rising

Trooper of the 13th Light Dragoons with M1812 uniform.

(1745–1748). It should be noted, however, that in Britain the introduction of new light cavalry tactics encountered very strong opposition: the British officer corps of the time, especially that of cavalry, was an extremely conservative one that considered as 'suspicious' any innovation coming from abroad. Over time, however, evidence obliged even the traditionalists to abandon their positions.

Until 1745, the British Army comprised only heavy cavalry units (horse regiments) and medium cavalry units (dragoon regiments). In that year, however, the second Jacobite Rising began in Scotland. During the rebellion, British mounted units experienced difficulties in capturing the highly mobile insurgent forces of the Highlanders, who moved very rapidly on the broken terrain of the Highlands and were masters in employing hit-and-run tactics. As a result, the Duke of Kingston, an English noble who supported the British military efforts against the Jacobites, decided to raise a volunteer horse regiment that had light cavalry training from his land possessions in Nottinghamshire. This new corps, organized by the duke at his own expense, was officially ranked as the 10th Regiment of Horse of the British Army, but its members were trained as light cavalrymen despite being equipped and uniformed like standard heavy horsemen. The Duke of Kingston's Regiment of Horse performed extremely well fighting the Jacobites, including at the decisive Battle of Culloden, after which it pursued the defeated Jacobites with great determination. Initially, the regulars of the British Army had many prejudices about this new light corps, but combat experience showed them the potential of the new unit. After the suppression of the Jacobite Rising, in 1746, the 'experimental' volunteer regiment raised by the Duke of Kingston was disbanded, its members having enlisted only for the duration of the conflict. The Duke of Cumberland, who had commanded the British Army at the Battle of Culloden, had a very positive opinion of this unit and would have preferred to retain it in service. Although this was not possible for practical reasons, the Duke found a way to maintain some light cavalry. He organized a new light cavalry unit, known as the Duke of Cumberland's Regiment of Light Dragoons, in which he enlisted all the men of the recently disbanded Duke of Kingston's Regiment of Horse. The new corps was the first regular light cavalry unit ever formed by the British Army, and was the first to be ranked as Light Dragoons.

The regiment was soon dispatched to continental Europe, participating in the final operations of the War of the Austrian Succession, distinguishing itself at the Battle of Lauffeld. In 1749, however, the Duke of Cumberland's Regiment of Light Dragoons was disbanded soon after the end of the hostilities in Europe. The Duke of Cumberland was one of the first British military officers to understand the importance and the potential of the new light cavalry corps. During the Jacobite Uprising, for example, he had a small personal bodyguard formed by a few hussars who were recruited in Hungary. These, despite being just a few men, fought with distinction at Culloden, and gave a good impression to even the most traditionalist officers of the British Army. These 'Duke of Cumberland's Hussars' were the first unit of the British Army to wear the traditional dress of the Hungarian light cavalry. Until 1757, the British cavalry continued to be made up only of horse regiments and dragoon regiments, since the experimental cavalry corps active from 1745–1749 were all disbanded with the end of the ongoing wars. It seemed just a question of time, however, before Britain would be involved in a new conflict. Indeed, several years later the Seven Years' War broke out and the British Army found itself involved in a new large-scale European war. The need for light cavalry units was becoming increasingly strong in all the major armies of the time, and the British Army was no exception to this rule. In April 1757, the formation of a total of eleven independent troops of light cavalry was authorized, each of which was attached to one of the existing horse regiments and had the following internal establishment: three officers, one troop quartermaster, five NCOs, two drummers and sixty troopers. Members of these new troops were chosen from the youngest and fittest recruits of the existing horse regiments. They were mounted on small and nimble horses, being trained to act as skirmishers and explorers. The new light horsemen continued to wear the standard uniforms of their parent regiments, but received a distinctive headgear: a black leather helmet with an upright comb, a frontal plate mounted with brass and a drooping feather. They were still armed with straight-bladed swords, but also carried a flintlock carbine and a couple of pistols. The glorious tradition of the British Light Dragoons was born: within a few years, these new light cavalry showed their great potential, to the point that in 1759 it was decided to form seven completely independent regiments of light cavalry.

These regiments were recruited very rapidly and were numbered in progressive order after the fourteen regiments of dragoons that existed at the time. The following new units of Light Dragoons were organized:

- **15th Regiment of Light Dragoons:** Raised in the London area by George Augustus Eliott, the regiment soon distinguished itself during the Battle of Emsdorf (1760) in Germany. After taking part in the Battle of Wilhelmsthal (1762), they returned home. Between 1766 and 1769, there was an attempt to give a separate numeration to the regiments of Light Dragoons, and thus the unit became the 1st Regiment of Light Dragoons. When this experiment ended, however, the corps reverted to its original denomination.
- **16th Regiment of Light Dragoons:** This unit, raised by John Burgoyne, took part in the final operations of the Seven Years' War. From 1766–1769, it was named as 2nd Regiment of Light Dragoons.

- **17th Regiment of Light Dragoons:** Raised in Scotland, they were disbanded at the end of the Seven Years' War.
- **18th Regiment of Light Dragoons:** This unit saw some action in Germany during 1761, and was renamed as the 3rd Regiment of Light Dragoons in 1766. In 1769, it was ranked as the 17th Regiment of Light Dragoons since the unit originally having that denomination had been disbanded.
- **19th Regiment of Light Dragoons:** Renamed as the 4th Regiment of Light Dragoons in 1766, during 1769 it was ranked as the 18th Regiment of Light Dragoons. It was formed by brigading some of the light troops that had been created in 1757.
- **20th Regiment of Light Dragoons:** Raised in Ireland, the unit was disbanded at the end of the Seven Years' War. It was formed by brigading some of the light troops that had been created in 1757.
- **21st Regiment of Light Dragoons:** Raised in England, the regiment was disbanded at the end of the Seven Years' War. It was created by brigading some of the light troops that had been formed in 1757.

By 1765, the British cavalry comprised a total of four regiments of Light Dragoons, which were augmented to five in 1768 when the 12th Regiment of Dragoons became the 12th Regiment of Light Dragoons. The combat experiences of the Seven Years' War had shown the importance of having some good light cavalry, so when the American Revolution began, the British government decided to expand its own mounted troops by adding more light cavalry corps as follows:

- **19th Regiment of Light Dragoons:** raised in 1779, disbanded in 1783.
- **20th Regiment of Light Dragoons:** raised in 1779, disbanded in 1783.
- **21st Regiment of Light Dragoons:** raised in 1779, disbanded in 1783.
- **22nd Regiment of Light Dragoons:** raised in 1779, disbanded in 1783.
- **23rd Regiment of Light Dragoons:** raised in 1781, not disbanded.

As is clear from the above, most of these new units were temporary corps with a very short history, the only exception being the 23rd Regiment, which became the new 19th Light Dragoons when the latter was disbanded in 1783. Nevertheless, the British light cavalry distinguished itself in North America, clearly showing its superiority when confronted by the mounted troops deployed by the Thirteen Colonies. The broken terrain of North America did not permit the use of large cavalry units and limited the movement of all mounted soldiers with heavy personal equipment. Consequently, the Light Dragoons were the only horse soldiers who

Officer of the 14th Light Dragoons with M1812 dress.

Trooper of the 15th Light Dragoons with M1807 uniform.

could operate effectively in that theatre of operations. Of the several light cavalry units that were part of the British Army between 1775 and 1783, only two – the 16th and 17th Light Dragoons – served in North America and thus could learn from their combat experience in the American Revolution.

In addition to the creation of the new short-lived units listed above, the years of the American Revolution also saw the transformation of the following existing heavy cavalry corps into regiments of Light Dragoons:

- The 7th Regiment of Dragoons became the **7th Regiment of Light Dragoons** in 1783.
- The 8th Regiment of Dragoons became the **8th Regiment of Light Dragoons** in 1776.
- The 9th Regiment of Dragoons became the **9th Regiment of Light Dragoons** in 1783.
- The 10th Regiment of Dragoons became the **10th Regiment of Light Dragoons** in 1783.
- The 11th Regiment of Dragoons became the **11th Regiment of Light Dragoons** in 1783.
- The 13th Regiment of Dragoons became the **13th Regiment of Light Dragoons** in 1783.
- The 14th Regiment of Dragoons became the **14th Regiment of Light Dragoons** in 1776.

These seven units obtained by converting regiments of dragoons remained in service after the end of the American Revolution, so by 1785, the British cavalry comprised a total of thirteen light units (numbered 7–19, in progressive order after the six remaining regiments of dragoons). With the outbreak of the Revolutionary Wars, the expansion of the British light cavalry continued with the creation of the following new units (many of which were short-lived):

- **20th Regiment of Light Dragoons:** raised in 1792, disbanded in 1818.
- **21st Regiment of Light Dragoons:** raised in 1794, disbanded in 1819.
- **22nd Regiment of Light Dragoons:** raised in 1794, disbanded in 1802.
- **23rd Regiment of Light Dragoons:** raised in 1794, disbanded in 1802.
- **24th Regiment of Light Dragoons:** raised in 1794, disbanded in 1802.
- **25th Regiment of Light Dragoons:** raised in 1794, it later became the 22nd Light Dragoons and was disbanded in 1820.
- **26th Regiment of Light Dragoons:** raised in 1794, it later became the 23rd Light Dragoons and was disbanded in 1817.

- **27th Regiment of Light Dragoons:** raised in 1794, it later became the 24th Light Dragoons and was disbanded in 1819.
- **28th Regiment of Light Dragoons:** raised in 1794, disbanded in 1802.
- **29th Regiment of Light Dragoons:** raised in 1794, it later became the 25th Light Dragoons and was disbanded in 1819.
- **30th Regiment of Light Dragoons:** raised in 1794, disbanded in 1796.
- **31st Regiment of Light Dragoons:** raised in 1794, disbanded in 1796.
- **32nd Regiment of Light Dragoons:** raised in 1794, disbanded in 1796.
- **33rd Regiment of Light Dragoons:** raised in 1794, disbanded in 1796.

As a result of the above, the British cavalry included a total of nineteen regiments of Light Dragoons in 1803. As we will see from the regimental histories of these units, the Light Dragoons were a fundamental component of the British Army that fought against Napoleon from 1800–1815. They formed the bulk of the British mounted troops and were sent to fight overseas much more frequently than the heavy cavalry regiments. Thanks to their tactical flexibility, they could be used to perform a variety of tasks and could operate on any kind of terrain. During the early years of the Napoleonic Wars, the French hussars obtained a series of brilliant victories and became famous for their incredible courage as well as their ornate uniforms. The British Army also fell victim to the French hussars' vogue, and thus in 1806 and 1807 some of its Light Dragoon regiments were transformed into hussar units. In total, four units were involved in such conversions: the 7th, 10th, 15th and 18th Light Dragoons. The transformation of these units into hussar regiments did not affect their training and tactical functions; nor did it change their progressive number, but simply saw the introduction of new and much more costly hussar-style uniforms. Shortly after the Battle of Waterloo, during which the British officers were impressed by the combat capabilities of the French lancers, three regiments of Light Dragoons (the 9th, 12th and 16th) were transformed into lancer units.

Generally speaking, the British Light Dragoons did not improve their combat capabilities in any significant way between 1770 and 1792. By the outbreak of the Revolutionary Wars, they operated like the rest of the British cavalry and had retained very little of their original 'light' nature. To deal with this problem and improve the general quality of the light mounted units, as early as 1778, a *Discipline of the Light Horse* had been published by Captain Hinde. This contained a mass of detailed information regarding the training and equipment of the light horsemen, but unfortunately for the British Light Dragoons, it did not have any great diffusion and was never put into practice. At Wellington's orders, especially in the Iberian Peninsula, the British light mounted troops learned a lot from their experience.

What follows are brief regimental histories of the Light Dragoon regiments:

From the left, officer of the 15th Light Dragoons, officer of the 18th Light Dragoons, trumpeter of the 18th Light Dragoons and trooper of the 18th Light Dragoons. They are all wearing M1807 dress.

7th Regiment of Light Dragoons: Raised as a dragoon regiment in 1690 as part of the Scots Army, during the latter's expansion ordered by William of Orange after the Glorious Revolution. They participated in the War of the Grand Alliance and the War of the Spanish Succession in continental Europe, and later fought in the Jacobite Rising of 1715, taking part in the Battle of Sheriffmuir. During the War of the Austrian Succession, the unit fought in the battles of Dettingen, Fontenoy, Rocoux and Lauffeld. In 1760, the regiment took part in the Battle of Warburg during the Seven Years' War. In 1783, the unit was converted into a regiment of Light

Dragoons and as such was sent to Flanders in order to fight against Revolutionary France. It was transformed into a hussar unit in 1807, and during the following year it was sent to the Iberian Peninsula to fight under Sir John Moore. After the end of that unfortunate campaign, which saw the French invasion of Portugal, the 7th Hussars remained in Britain until 1813, when they were again sent to the Iberian Peninsula. The regiment participated in the Battle of Orthes in southern France before being despatched home in 1814. When Napoleon returned from exile in Elba, the regiment fought with distinction in the Belgian campaign and at the Battle of Waterloo.

8th Regiment of Light Dragoons: Raised during 1693 in Ireland, the regiment fought as a dragoon unit in the War of the Spanish Succession, suffering heavy losses. After having been completely reorganized, it was involved in the crushing of the Jacobite Rising of 1715. The corps returned to Scotland at the outbreak of the second Jacobite Rising in 1745, and it was transformed into a regiment of Light Dragoons in 1776. It took part in the Flanders campaign that was fought against Revolutionary France, before being despatched to India in 1802, where it fought in several important military actions against the Marathas and the Gurkhas. The unit returned to Europe only in 1819, after having been converted into a hussar corps.

9th Regiment of Light Dragoons: This unit was created during the Jacobite Rising of 1715 as part of the British military response to the Scottish revolt. After many years spent in Ireland performing garrison duties, it ceased to be a regiment of dragoons and was converted into a unit of Light Dragoons (1783). During 1798, the corps participated with distinction in the suppression of the Irish Revolt. In 1806 and 1807, it took part in the disastrous British military expedition against the Spanish colonies of South America (Argentina and Uruguay), then in 1809, it participated in the unfortunate Walcheren campaign during which many of its members died of fever. The unit was later sent to the Iberian Peninsula, where it fought in several actions during 1811 and 1812. In 1813, the 9th Regiment returned to Britain and performed garrison duties until the end of the Napoleonic Wars. The corps was transformed into a regiment of lancers in 1816.

10th Regiment of Light Dragoons: This unit was created during the Jacobite Rising of 1715, as part of the British military response to the Scottish revolt. It then remained on garrison duty in Cornwall for twenty-five years until being despatched to Scotland in 1745 to fight once more against the Jacobites. During the Seven Years' War, it was sent for the first time to continental Europe, participating with distinction to the clashes at Minden (1759) and Warburg (1760). In 1783, the corps was transformed into a regiment of Light Dragoons but did not take part in any military campaigns until being converted into a hussar unit in 1807. During the following year, it was sent to the Iberian Peninsula, where it fought under Sir John Moore. Before returning to Britain, it fought with distinction at the Battle of Benavente, during which it captured the commander of the French cavalry (General Lefebvre-Desnouettes). In 1813, the regiment was sent back to the Iberian Peninsula, and during the following year it took part in Wellington's invasion of southern France. It was part of the British forces that were deployed in Belgium in 1815, and charged against the French at Waterloo.

11th Regiment of Light Dragoons: Also created as a dragoon unit during the Jacobite Rising of 1715, the regiment remained on garrison duty in Scotland for several years and participated in the defeat of the 1745 Jacobite Rising. In 1760, the corps was despatched to Germany to take part in the Seven Years' War and fought at the Battle of Warburg. In 1783, together with several other regiments, the unit was transformed into a corps of Light Dragoons. Small detachments of the 11th Light Dragoons participated in the Flanders campaign and to the later Anglo-Russian invasion of Holland (1799). In 1801, the unit was deployed for a brief period in Egypt, before remaining on garrison duty at home for several years. It was sent to the Iberian Peninsula in 1811, fighting at Badajoz and Salamanca (1812) before returning to Britain. In 1815, it was involved in the Belgian campaign and the Battle of Waterloo.

12th Regiment of Light Dragoons: This regiment was formed as a dragoon unit during the Jacobite Rising of 1715. Three years later, it was placed on the Irish establishment of the British Army and was sent to Ireland to act as a garrison unit. It operated as such for a very long period of 75 years, being transformed into a regiment of Light Dragoons in 1768. The unit finally saw some action in 1794, taking part in the attack against the French defences of Bastia in Corsica. In 1801, the regiment was sent to Egypt, where it fought at the Battle of Alexandria. After a few years spent in Britain, it was made part of the British expeditionary force that landed at Walcheren in the Netherlands in 1809. From 1811–1814, the 12th Light Dragoons served under Wellington in the Iberian Peninsula, distinguishing themselves at the Battle of Salamanca (1812). After a brief period spent in Britain, the regiment was sent to Belgium in 1815 and fought with determination at Waterloo. Soon after the end of hostilities, it was transformed into a unit of lancers.

13th Regiment of Light Dragoons: Raised during the military emergency caused by the Jacobite Rebellion of 1715, the regiment was later despatched to Ireland,

Officer of the 18th Light Dragoons with M1807 uniform.

where it remained on garrison duty until 1742. With the outbreak of the 1745 Jacobite Uprising, it was sent to Scotland, where it suffered heavy casualties during a series of minor clashes fought against the rebel Highlanders. After the end of the revolt, the unit was sent back to Ireland, where it was transformed into a regiment of Light Dragoons in 1783. A small detachment of the corps served in the West Indies between 1795 and 1798, but the unit did not see any major fighting for several years. In 1810, it was despatched to the Iberian Peninsula, where it served with distinction until 1814. After taking part in the invasion of southern France, the regiment was briefly sent back home. In 1815, with the return of Napoleon, the 13th Light Dragoons fought at Waterloo, conducting several charges against the enemy and suffering significant losses.

14th Regiment of Light Dragoons: Raised during the Jacobite Rebellion of 1715, the regiment was later despatched to Ireland, where it remained as part of the garrison until 1742. With the outbreak of the 1745 Jacobite Uprising, it was sent to Scotland, suffering severe casualties in minor clashes against the Highlanders. At the end of the revolt, the unit was sent back to Ireland, where it was transformed into a regiment of Light Dragoons in 1776. Two of the unit's troops participated in the Flanders campaign, while seven were sent to the West Indies in 1795 to support the Haitian Revolution against the French. In 1808, the 14th Light Dragoons were sent to the Iberian Peninsula, where they remained until 1814. The regiment soon proved to be one of the best cavalry corps of the British Army, taking part with distinction in several important clashes, including those at Salamanca and Vittoria. In the summer of 1814, after participating in the invasion of southern France, the unit went back to Britain for several months. However, two of its squadrons were despatched to North America, when the ongoing War of 1812 between Great Britain and the USA entered its final stage. The detachment of the 14th Light Dragoons fought at the bloody Battle of New Orleans in 1815, which was one of the worst defeats suffered by the British Army during this period.

15th Regiment of Light Dragoons: Created as a Light Dragoon regiment in 1759, it was soon sent to continental Europe to participate in the Seven Years' War. The unit distinguished itself during the Battle of Emsdorf (1760) and also took part in the Battle of Wilhelmsthal (1762) before returning home. In 1793, it was sent to Flanders, where it fought against the French on several occasions. During 1799, the corps was made part of the British expeditionary force that participated in the unsuccessful Anglo-Russian invasion of Holland. In 1807, the regiment was converted into a hussar corps, and as such it was sent to the Iberian Peninsula in 1808. During the

Trumpeter of the 18th Light Dragoons with M1807 dress.

following year, the 15th Light Dragoons returned home, before returning to Spain in 1813. They participated in the decisive Battle of Vittoria and the ensuing invasion of southern France (fighting at Orthes and Toulouse). In 1815, the corps took part in the Belgian campaign and was present at Waterloo. A few years after the end of the Napoleonic Wars, in 1819, the regiment charged against a protesting crowd during the so-called Peterloo Massacre at Manchester.

16th Regiment of Light Dragoons: Formed as a Light Dragoon regiment in 1759, they participated in the Seven Years' War and were sent to Portugal to support the country's military efforts against Spain. In 1776, the unit was despatched to the Thirteen Colonies to combat the American Revolution; during which it took part in several important engagements: Brandywine (1777), Germantown (1777) and Monmouth (1778). The regiment returned to Britain in 1779. With the outbreak of the Revolutionary Wars with France, the 16th Light Dragoons were despatched to Flanders, where they took part in several engagements before being sent home in 1796. After a period performing garrison duties in Ireland, the regiment was despatched to the Iberian Peninsula in 1809. In Spain, the soldiers of the corps distinguished themselves at several battles: Talavera (1809), Bussaco (1810), Salamanca (1812) and Vittoria (1813). With the return of Napoleon from his exile on Elba, the unit fought in the Belgian campaign of 1815 and was at the Battle of Waterloo.

17th Regiment of Light Dragoons: Raised as a Light Dragoon regiment in 1759, it was sent to North America in 1775 and was the only cavalry unit of the British Army that participated in military operations throughout the American Revolution. In 1777, a detachment from the regiment was used to create the infamous 'British Legion' commanded by Banastre Tarleton, which fought with counter-guerrilla methods against the American insurgents and obtained a series of minor victories during the central years of the conflict. After the end of the hostilities in North America, the 17th Light Dragoons returned home and were assigned to garrison duty in Ireland. In 1795, two of their troops were sent to the West Indies in order to crush some local revolts. The regiment took part in the disastrous British military expedition against the Spanish colonies of South America (Argentina and Uruguay) in 1806 and 1807. In 1808, the corps was sent to India, where it remained until the end of the Napoleonic Wars.

18th Regiment of Light Dragoons: Organized as a Light Dragoon regiment in 1759, it was sent to the West Indies in order to fight against the French in 1796 and 1797. In 1799, it took part in the unfortunate Anglo-Russian invasion of Holland, during which it fought at the Battle of Bergen. In 1808, the unit was despatched to the Iberian Peninsula after having been converted into a hussar corps during the previous year. The 18th Light Dragoons returned to Britain in 1809, but in 1813 they were sent back to Spain. They fought with Wellington at the Battle of Vittoria. In 1814, the unit spent some months at home, before being sent to Belgium when Napoleon returned to France. It fought at the Battle of Waterloo, during which it charged against the French.

19th Regiment of Light Dragoons: This unit was created in 1781 specifically for service in India. At that time, the fledgling British Empire did not have any European cavalry corps in the Indian sub-continent, so the regiment became the first unit of the regular British cavalry to serve in India. It participated with distinction to the Anglo-Mysore Wars and the Anglo-Maratha Wars, before fighting at the decisive Battle of Assaye (1803) under the command of a young Wellington. In 1806, the 19th Light Dragoons returned to Britain and performed garrison duties until the outbreak of hostilities with the USA. In 1812, they were sent to North America, where they remained until 1816, being the only cavalry unit of the British Army that participated throughout the War of 1812. The regiment fought with great professionalism in North America, acting as the main cavalry unit of the British Army. In 1816 it was re-equipped as a corps of lancers.

20th Regiment of Light Dragoons: Raised in 1792, this unit was created specifically for service in Jamaica. Its main task was to suppress the activities of the many maroons who attacked the British plantations on the island. In 1807, the corps, after many years of service in the West Indies, took part in the disastrous British expedition against the Spanish colonies of Argentina and Uruguay in South America. During that same year, one squadron of the regiment participated in the Alexandria Expedition, a punitive raid against Ottoman Egypt and one of Britain's lesser-known military operations of the Napoleonic Wars. In 1808, the 20th Light Dragoons were sent to the Iberian Peninsula, where they fought at the Battle of Vimeiro before returning home. The unit was disbanded in 1818 during the great demobilization that took place after the end of the Napoleonic period.

21st Regiment of Light Dragoons: Formed in 1794 and commonly known as the Yorkshire Light Dragoons, this was a very short-lived corps that was disbanded in 1819 after having spent the entire period of the Napoleonic Wars in Ireland.

22nd Regiment of Light Dragoons: Raised in 1794 for service in India, this unit took part in the British occupation of Java during 1811 and remained on the garrison

Trooper of the 23rd Light Dragoons with M1812 uniform.

of the island until 1813. After the annexation of the Netherlands to the French Empire in 1811, the British government had decided to occupy the Dutch colonial territories of present-day Indonesia in order to prevent the French from obtaining direct control over them. Java, the most important of the Dutch colonial possessions, was invaded in 1811 by a British expeditionary force organized in India. The island was returned to the Netherlands only at the end of the Napoleonic Wars. A few years later, in 1820, the 22nd Regiment of Light Dragoons was disbanded.

23rd Regiment of Light Dragoons: After being raised in 1794, this unit served with great distinction during the Napoleonic Wars. Its first major deployment overseas was in Egypt, where the British and the Ottomans fought against the French, obtaining a complete victory in 1801. With the outbreak of the Peninsular War, the corps was sent to Spain, where it participated in several engagements and fought with great determination at the Battle of Talavera (1809). After a brief period spent in Britain, the 23rd Light Dragoons took part in the Belgian campaign of 1815 and fought at Waterloo. The regiment was disbanded in 1817.

24th Regiment of Light Dragoons: Raised in 1794 for service in India, this regiment participated in the Second Anglo-Maratha War and was never sent back to Britain until being finally disbanded in 1819.

25th Regiment of Light Dragoons: This regiment was also raised in 1794 for service in India, taking part in the Second Anglo-Maratha War. It too was never sent back to Britain until being disbanded in 1819. In 1810, one of the troops from the regiment took part in the British occupation of Mauritius (at that time a French colony).

26th Regiment of Light Dragoons: This was one of the eight regiments of Light Dragoons raised in 1794 as part of the great mobilization that took place after the outbreak of hostilities with Revolutionary France. It was disbanded in 1802 following the Peace of Amiens, without having seen action.

27th Regiment of Light Dragoons: One of the eight regiments of Light Dragoons raised as part of the great mobilization that took place in 1794 after the outbreak of war with Revolutionary France. It was disbanded in 1802 following the Peace of Amiens, never having seen action.

28th Regiment of Light Dragoons: Another of the eight regiments of Light Dragoons raised in 1794 as part of the major mobilization after the outbreak of

General of the Light Dragoons wearing M1812 dress.

hostilities with Revolutionary France. It was disbanded in 1802 following the Peace of Amiens, without having seen action.

29th Regiment of Light Dragoons: One of the eight regiments of Light Dragoons raised as part of the great mobilization in 1794 at the outbreak of war with Revolutionary France. Following the Peace of Amiens, it was disbanded in 1802 without having seen action.

30th Regiment of Light Dragoons: This was one of the eight regiments of Light Dragoons raised in 1794 as part of the great mobilization that took place after the outbreak of hostilities with Revolutionary France. It was disbanded in 1796 after the end of the Flanders campaign, without having seen action.

31st Regiment of Light Dragoons: One of the eight regiments of Light Dragoons raised in 1794 as part of the mass mobilization after the outbreak of hostilities with Revolutionary France. It was disbanded in 1796 following the end of the Flanders campaign, never having seen action.

32nd Regiment of Light Dragoons: Yet another of the eight regiments of Light Dragoons raised in 1794 in the great mobilization after the outbreak of hostilities with Revolutionary France. It was disbanded in 1796 following the end of the Flanders campaign, without having seen action.

33rd Regiment of Light Dragoons: The last of the eight regiments of Light Dragoons raised in 1794 under the major mobilization that took place after the outbreak of hostilities with Revolutionary France. Following the end of the Flanders campaign, it was disbanded in 1796 without having seen action.

The internal organization of the regiments of Light Dragoons changed very little during the Napoleonic era. They were structured on ten troops each, two of which made up a squadron. Squadrons were known by numbers, with troops known by letters (the opposite of what was the case with the heavy cavalry regiments). Of the five squadrons, one was a depot unit that was always kept in reserve in Britain and was never sent to serve overseas. The depot squadron of each regiment provided new recruits with solid basic training for the four active squadrons in order to replenish the losses suffered during overseas deployments. In 1813, two additional troops were added to each regiment of Light Dragoons in order to form a fifth active squadron. The regimental staff of the light cavalry units comprised the following elements:

Trooper of the KGL's 1st Light Dragoons with M1807 uniform.

one colonel, two lieutenant colonels, two majors, six captains, one captain lieutenant, eight lieutenants, nine cornets, one paymaster, one adjutant, one surgeon, two assistant surgeons and one veterinary surgeon. Each troop included the following: one lieutenant colonel, one major, one captain, one quartermaster, four sergeants, four corporals, one trumpeter and ninety troopers. In June 1809, the quartermaster of each troop was transformed into a sergeant-major, and a lieutenant quartermaster was added to the staff of each regiment. During 1810, the internal composition of a light cavalry unit's regimental staff was slightly modified to became the following: one colonel, one lieutenant-colonel, one major, one adjutant, one lieutenant quartermaster, one paymaster, one surgeon, two assistant surgeons, one veterinary surgeon and one regimental sergeant major. The new composition of a single troop was as follows: one captain, one lieutenant, one cornet, one troop sergeant major, three sergeants, four corporals, one trumpeter, one farrier and sixty-three troopers. By 1809, the average numerical consistency of most light cavalry regiments was 905 officers and men. The units that transformed into hussar corps retained their previous internal organization.

Uniforms and equipment

The British Light Dragoons used three different uniforms during the Napoleonic era. The first was adopted in 1784, shortly after the end of the American Revolution, and consisted of a fur-crested Tarleton helmet worn together with a short-tailed sleeved waistcoat and a sleeveless shell-jacket. Both the latter garments were in dark blue. Until 1784, the Light Dragoons had been dressed in red like the rest of the British cavalry, and the only peculiar element of their uniforms was the black leather helmet (the heavy cavalry had the more traditional bicorn as headgear). With the new dress regulations of 1784, it was decided to differentiate the Light Dragoons from the rest of the British cavalry in a more apparent way. In 1796, however, this uniform was substituted by a new one, which was of clear 'hussar' cut: the braided sleeved waistcoat was abolished and the shell-jacket was modified in order to become a hussar's dolman, which had sleeves and no tails. The headgear remained the same, since the Tarleton helmet was extremely popular among the rankers. In 1807, some regiments of Light Dragoons were converted into hussar units and thus received new uniforms, which were extremely costly to produce but very elegant. These included hussar-style dolman and pelisse and had a busby covered with fur as headgear. The dolman and pelisse both derived from the traditional dress of the Magyar hussars, since the first light cavalrymen of this type had appeared in Hungary. The dolman was a jacket cut tight and short, decorated with multiple rows of buttons (usually three) and with some stripes of frogging on the front. The pelisse was a short fur-trimmed jacket that was worn hanging loose over the left shoulder. In 1812, the

Light Dragoons received a new uniform, quite different from that previously worn, which remained in use until the end of the Napoleonic Wars. This included a black shako as headgear instead of the Tarleton helmet, and consisted of a dark blue tunic with coloured frontal plastron and short tails. The tunic of this M1812 dress was criticized by several British officers, including Wellington, because its colour and cut were too similar to those worn by the contemporary French cavalry. In particular, the new tunic looked very similar to the kurtka (short-tailed tunic with frontal plastron) of the Imperial Guard's Polish Lancers.

Trooper of the KGL's 3rd Light Dragoons with M1807 dress.

The M1784 uniform of the Light Dragoons was as follows: black leather Tarleton helmet with black peak, black fur crest, plume in regimental colour (worn on the left side), band wrapped around the bottom part in regimental colour, cockade on the back in regimental colour and white metal unit badge (worn on the right side); dark blue sleeveless shell jacket with collar in regimental colour piped in white, white frontal frogging and white piping to the front and bottom edges; dark blue short-tailed sleeved waistcoat with pointed cuffs in regimental colour piped in white, shoulder straps in regimental colour piped in white and additional white braiding on the buttonholes of the waistcoat's front; white trousers, black leather boots and white belt equipment. The officers wore the same uniform, but with all the white elements in silver. In addition, they had a red sash worn around the waist and instead of the shoulder straps they had shoulder wings covered with silver scales. The regiments of Light Dragoons that were raised for service in India wore a peculiar version of this same dress: black leather Tarleton helmet with black peak, black fur crest, plume in regimental colour (worn on the left side), band wrapped around the bottom part in regimental colour, cockade on the back in regimental colour and white metal unit badge (worn on the right side); light blue-grey sleeveless shell jacket with collar in regimental colour piped in white, white frontal frogging and white piping to the front and bottom edges; light blue-grey short-tailed sleeved waistcoat with pointed cuffs in regimental colour piped in white, shoulder straps in regimental colour piped in white and additional white braiding on the buttonholes of the waistcoat's front; white trousers, black leather short boots and white leather belt equipment.

The M1796 uniform of the Light Dragoons comprised the following elements: black leather Tarleton helmet with black peak, black fur crest, plume in regimental colour (worn on the left side), band wrapped around the bottom part in regimental colour, cockade on the back in regimental colour and white metal unit badge (worn on the right side); dark blue dolman with collar and pointed cuffs in regimental colour, both piped in white; shoulder wings in regimental colour with white piping, white frontal frogging with three rows of vertical buttons, and white decorative Hungarian knots embroidered on the pointed cuffs and front of the trousers; dark blue trousers, black leather short boots with frontal tassel and white leather belt equipment. In 1796, the Light Dragoons also received a sabretache small bag, which was part of the contemporary hussar dress and was used to transport documents. The officers wore the same uniform described above, but with all the white elements in silver. In addition, they had a red sash worn around the waist and their Hungarian knots (embroidered on the cuffs and trousers) were more complex according to their rank. The regiments of Light Dragoons serving in India wore a peculiar version of this same dress: black leather Tarleton helmet with black peak, black fur crest,

From the left, trooper of the KGL's 1st Light Dragoons, trooper of the KGL's 2nd Light Dragoons, officer of the KGL's 1st Light Dragoons and officer of the KGL's 2nd Light Dragoons. They are all wearing M1812 uniform.

plume in regimental colour (worn on the left side), band wrapped around the bottom part in regimental colour, cockade on the back in regimental colour and white metal unit badge (worn on the right side); light blue-grey dolman with collar and pointed cuffs in regimental colour, both piped in white; shoulder wings in regimental colour with white piping, white frontal frogging with three rows of vertical buttons, and white decorative Hungarian knots embroidered on the pointed cuffs and front of the trousers; light blue-grey trousers, black leather short boots with frontal tassel and white leather belt equipment.

The M1807 uniform adopted by those regiments that were converted into hussar units was as follows: tall busby covered with brown fur having white cords, white-and-red short plume and red soft 'bag' on the right side; dark blue dolman with collar and cuffs in regimental colour, both piped in white; white frontal frogging with three rows of buttons, white piping to front and bottom edges, and white Hungarian knots embroidered on the sleeves; dark blue pelisse lined with fur, having white frontal frogging and white piping to the cuffs; wrapped sash around the waist, in two different colours that varied for each regiment; white trousers, black leather short boots with frontal tassel and white leather belt equipment. The hussars also received the sabretache bag, but their model was not entirely black like that of the Light Dragoons, in their case being decorated with ornate embroidering that reproduced the unit badge of each regiment. Officers were dressed like their men, but the white elements of the dress were all silver for them, while the cords of the busby were golden and not white. In 1812, a new model of busby was introduced, which was gradually adopted by all the hussar regiments by 1815; this was shorter but larger compared with the previous one, and had yellow cords instead of white and a brass chinscale.

The M1812 uniform of the Light Dragoons comprised the following elements: black shako with white/yellow top band, white/yellow frontal pompom, white-and-red short plume, white/yellow cords, black leather peak, brass chinscale and black cockade with white/yellow external edge; dark blue tunic with collar and pointed cuffs in regimental colour, frontal plastron in regimental colour, white epaulettes on the shoulders, piping to the rear seams of the tunic in regimental colour, short turnbacks in regimental colour and dark blue pockets piped in regimental colour on the back of the turnbacks; sash wrapped around the waist in dark blue with regimental colour; grey trousers with red double side-stripe, black leather short boots, black leather sabretache and white leather belt equipment. On campaign, the trousers had a black or brown internal leather reinforcement. Officers were dressed similarly to their men, but with several elements of their uniform in gold: black shako with golden top band, golden frontal pompom, white-and-red short plume, golden cords, black leather peak, brass chinscale and black cockade with golden external edge;

dark blue tunic with collar and pointed cuffs in regimental colour, frontal plastron in regimental colour, golden shoulder epaulettes, piping to the rear seams of the tunic in regimental colour, short turnbacks in regimental colour and dark blue pockets piped in regimental colour on the back of the turnbacks; sash wrapped around the waist, in gold and regimental colour; grey trousers with golden single side-stripe, black leather short boots, black leather sabretache and white leather belt equipment.

The regimental colours of the Light Dragoons units, which did not change during the period taken into account, were as follows:

- 7th Regiment of Light Dragoons: white
- 8th Regiment of Light Dragoons: scarlet red
- 9th Regiment of Light Dragoons: pale buff
- 10th Regiment of Light Dragoons: yellow
- 11th Regiment of Light Dragoons: pale buff
- 12th Regiment of Light Dragoons: pale yellow
- 13th Regiment of Light Dragoons: pale buff
- 14th Regiment of Light Dragoons: lemon yellow
- 15th Regiment of Light Dragoons: scarlet red
- 16th Regiment of Light Dragoons: scarlet red
- 17th Regiment of Light Dragoons: white
- 18th Regiment of Light Dragoons: white
- 19th Regiment of Light Dragoons: yellow
- 20th Regiment of Light Dragoons: yellow
- 21st Regiment of Light Dragoons: yellow
- 22nd Regiment of Light Dragoons: scarlet red
- 23rd Regiment of Light Dragoons: blue
- 24th Regiment of Light Dragoons: white
- 25th Regiment of Light Dragoons: buff
- 26th Regiment of Light Dragoons: blue
- 27th Regiment of Light Dragoons: white
- 28th Regiment of Light Dragoons: yellow
- 29th Regiment of Light Dragoons: buff
- 30th Regiment of Light Dragoons: blue
- 31st Regiment of Light Dragoons: yellow
- 32nd Regiment of Light Dragoons: blue
- 33rd Regiment of Light Dragoons: blue

Officer of the KGL's 2nd Light Dragoons with M1812 dress.

From the left, officer of the KGL's 1st Hussars, officer of the KGL's 2nd Hussars, officer of the KGL's 3rd Hussars and trooper of the KGL's 3rd Hussars. They are all wearing the new M1813 hussar uniform.

From 1812, the piping colour of the various units could be white or yellow and helped to distinguish the corps having the same regimental colour, according to the following scheme:

- 7th Regiment of Light Dragoons: white
- 8th Regiment of Light Dragoons: white
- 9th Regiment of Light Dragoons: white
- 10th Regiment of Light Dragoons: white
- 11th Regiment of Light Dragoons: white
- 12th Regiment of Light Dragoons: white
- 13th Regiment of Light Dragoons: yellow
- 14th Regiment of Light Dragoons: white
- 15th Regiment of Light Dragoons: white
- 16th Regiment of Light Dragoons: white
- 17th Regiment of Light Dragoons: white
- 18th Regiment of Light Dragoons: white
- 19th Regiment of Light Dragoons: white
- 20th Regiment of Light Dragoons: white
- 21st Regiment of Light Dragoons: white
- 22nd Regiment of Light Dragoons: white
- 23rd Regiment of Light Dragoons: white
- 24th Regiment of Light Dragoons: white
- 25th Regiment of Light Dragoons: white
- 26th Regiment of Light Dragoons: white
- 27th Regiment of Light Dragoons: white
- 28th Regiment of Light Dragoons: white
- 29th Regiment of Light Dragoons: white
- 30th Regiment of Light Dragoons: yellow
- 31st Regiment of Light Dragoons: white
- 32nd Regiment of Light Dragoons: white
- 33rd Regiment of Light Dragoons: white

Until 1812, the shabraque of the Light Dragoons was in regimental colour, with the royal monogram embroidered in a contrasting colour on the back corner and on pistol holsters; on the external edge it had a band in contrasting colour with a line of piping in the centre. In 1812, a new shabraque was introduced: this was dark blue with the royal monogram embroidered in regimental colour on the back corner; on the external edge it had a band in regimental colour. Over the new shabraque, a protective black or white sheepskin was worn on most occasions. Hussar regiments had a different model of shabraque, dark blue with the royal monogram embroidered on the back corner and an indented band in regimental colour on the external edge. This was used in combination with a protective black or white sheepskin. Until 1812, the trumpeters of the Light Dragoons were dressed in the standard uniform of their regiment, but with reversed colours; in that year, they received the same dress as the ordinary troopers but were easily distinguishable on the battlefield since the plume of their shakos was entirely red.

Chapter 4

Artillery and Technical Corps

Until the beginning of the eighteenth century, the artillerymen of most European armies were required to fire their guns but were not equipped to defend themselves from enemy attacks. As a result, while on the battlefield they had to be escorted by infantrymen specifically charged to do so. Until 1716, with the creation of the Royal Artillery, the British Army did not comprise any permanent company/battery of artillery: temporary artillery trains were organized by the Ordnance Department only when needed, and were usually disbanded at the end of each campaign. In time of peace, dozens of professional gunners were at the service of the Ordnance Department, scattered across Britain and manning the guns of the various garrisons. In case of war, they were assembled to form a train and were supplemented with a number of civilian mattrosses and pioneers, the latter being semi-skilled civilian labourers who were contracted only for the duration of a campaign. The conductors of the carts that were used to move the artillery pieces were also all civilians. As a result of the above situation, the eighteenth century was a period of great change and of progressive professionalization for the British artillery and the smaller technical corps that supported it. The first two permanent companies/batteries of artillery of the British Army were organized in 1716, being structured for the first time as independent corps. While they only received the official denomination of Royal Artillery in 1720, in practice they were an autonomous military force from their creation. The two original companies were soon increased to four, and were assembled – at least from an administrative point of view – with the artillery companies that were part of the garrison in Gibraltar and Menorca from the end of the War of the Spanish Succession. As a result of these organizational changes, the Royal Regiment of Artillery was created in 1722. This had the numerical consistency of a single battalion, and its members quickly became famous for their personal preparation and professionalism.

From the outset, selection and promotion in the Royal Artillery were based on merit, and thus all the officer corps of this new branch of service were highly experienced and skilled. In 1741, in order to improve the general quality of all the artillerymen serving across the British Empire, a cadet company was formed at the Royal Military Academy at Woolwich, tasked with training not only the officers of the Royal Artillery Regiment, but also those artillery officers who served with the

Officer of the Royal Artillery with pre-1796 dress.

British East India Company. In 1757, the Royal Artillery Regiment was reorganized on two battalions with twelve companies each, but its expansion continued during the following decades. By 1780, it comprised the following sub-units: four active battalions with eight companies each, two invalid independent companies employed to perform garrison duties and a permanent military band. By 1803, when hostilities with France resumed, the Royal Artillery consisted of eight battalions with ten companies/batteries each; a 9th Battalion was raised in 1806 and a 10th Battalion in 1808. The various battalions were not employed on the field as complete units, since their companies/batteries were usually deployed as autonomous corps. When this happened, they were commonly known as brigades despite consisting of companies with just six pieces each. Attached to each brigade there was always a detachment of artillery drivers, which was tasked with moving the guns on the field. The standard establishment of a Royal Artillery company/battery/brigade comprised the following elements: two captains, two first lieutenants, one second lieutenant, four sergeants, four corporals, nine bombardiers, three drummers and 116 gunners. Of the six artillery pieces that were manned by a company/battery/brigade, on most occasions five were field guns and one was a howitzer. These were transported together with their limbers and several wagons that were essential for their correct functioning: eight ammunition wagons, three baggage wagons and one spare-wheel wagon. In addition, each artillery brigade had a field forge that was vital for repairing damaged pieces. A total of about 100 drivers and 200 draught animals were usually needed to move a single artillery battery. Generally speaking, the traditional foot artillery moved very slowly on the battlefields of the early nineteenth century and changed position very rarely during a field battle.

To go beyond the limits of the foot artillery that have been described above, during the Seven Years' War the Prussian monarch Frederick the Great developed a new form of artillery that would be capable of moving much more rapidly on the battlefield thanks to the use of lighter guns drawn by horses. Initially, Frederick's idea seemed to be a complete failure, being too innovative, but over time it became clear that the new horse-drawn artillery had an enormous tactical potential. Differently from the foot artillery, horse batteries could be deployed very easily to wherever on the battlefield their presence was needed. They could also support attacks launched by the cavalry since they could move at the same pace as the horsemen. Creating a new branch of service from scratch was not a simple matter: new and lighter guns, specifically designed for the horse batteries, had to be created, while both the artillerymen and the horses of the new mounted batteries had to undergo specific training. New horse-drawn carriages were developed and specific tactics for the employment of mounted artillery were formulated. By the outbreak of the French Revolution, horse artillery

Soldier of the Royal Artillery with pre-1796 uniform.

was already an established presence in most of the major European armies. Prussia, for example, had three companies of horse artillery in 1792. Several other nations followed Frederick the Great's example during the late eighteenth century and organized their own units of mounted artillery: Austria (in 1778), Hanover (1786), Denmark-Norway (1790), France (1791) and Sweden (1792).

The British Army was quite slow in forming its own first units of horse artillery, since two troops of this new branch of service were organized only during January 1793. It is interesting to note that, differently from those of the foot artillery, the batteries of the horse artillery were known as troops, not as companies. The internal organization of the new mounted batteries remained quite similar to that of the cavalry troops, and this was also apparent in the uniforms used by the horse artillerymen, that were clearly of 'light cavalry' cut. In November 1793, another two troops of horse artillery were organized and these, together with the two existing troops, showed their great tactical flexibility during the Flanders campaign. Each mounted battery was equipped with six 6-pdr horse-drawn guns. By 1801, the number of horse batteries in the British Army had been increased to seven, and continued to be expanded during the following years; there were twelve troops of mounted artillery by 1806 (this establishment was maintained until the end of the Napoleonic Wars). Each single troop of horse artillery comprised the following elements: one captain, one second captain, three lieutenants, two staff sergeants, three sergeants, three corporals, six bombardiers, eighty gunners, sixty drivers, one farrier, one carriage-smith, two shoeing-smiths, two collar-makers, one wheelwright and one trumpeter. As in the foot artillery companies, the bombardiers by now did not have any specific duty, and their rank corresponded to that of lance corporal. The gunners were mounted on horses, while the drivers sat on the carriages or limbers of the guns when their battery moved. Each horse battery was divided into three divisions with two guns each; in turn, these were divided into two subdivisions with one gun each. A single division was commanded by a lieutenant, while each subdivision was commanded by a sergeant or a corporal. A single troop could also be divided into two half-brigades with three guns each, commanded by the captain or the second captain. Differently from the foot batteries, which were commonly known by the name of their commander, the horse batteries were known by letters.

During the Napoleonic Wars, some detachments of the Royal Artillery started to be equipped with rockets instead of guns. Initially, these new weapons were not very popular in the British Army, but their effectiveness eventually became apparent. In India, in particular, the Royal Artillery employed rockets against the forces of the local native rulers and obtained a series of memorable victories thanks to the psychological impact that the new weapons had on the enemy. In 1813, two independent units of horse artillery armed with rockets were formed; these were commonly known as Rocket Troops and their members were dressed quite similarly to the standard horse artillerymen. A single troop equipped with rockets consisted of 172 soldiers and could carry 840 missiles, so it had a considerable firepower. The Rocket Troops, albeit still having an experimental nature, participated in several engagements during 1814 and 1815.

In 1793, the British Army decided to 'militarize' its artillery drivers, as until then they had been unreliable civilian contractors with no discipline or training to speak of. As a result, the new Corps of Royal Artillery Drivers was formed, which comprised not only soldiers but also the draught animals and wagons that were needed to transport artillery guns and associated materials. By 1808, the Corps of Royal Artillery Drivers, whose members were dressed quite similarly to the soldiers of the horse artillery, comprised a total of eight troops. Each of these troops deployed 450 drivers organized into five sections of ninety men each, with 104 assorted craftsmen, 945 draught horses and seventy-five riding horses. Each troop was commanded by a captain. By the end of the Napoleonic Wars, the Corps of Royal Artillery Drivers had been expanded to eleven troops, with a total of eighty-eight officers and 7,352 other ranks. The sections of the artillery drivers' troops were divided among the artillery companies, with one section being usually attached to each battery. Wellington was never particularly happy with his Corps of Royal Artillery Drivers, because its members sometimes lacked discipline and were not guided by expert officers. Consequently, in 1817, the Corps of Royal Artillery Drivers was temporarily absorbed into the Royal Artillery before being disbanded in 1822.

The Corps of Royal Engineers, like the Royal Artillery, was organized as a stable military unit only in 1716. Until then, the British Army had included only a few independent officers with specific engineering skills. The formation of an independent Corps of Engineers (the 'Royal' prefix was added in 1787), however, did not change the existing situation in a significant way: until the outbreak of the Napoleonic Wars, the British engineers continued to comprise just a few commissioned officers who had undergone specific technical training at Woolwich. In 1792, there were seventy-three such officers, a number that was progressively augmented so that by 1813, the Corps of Royal Engineers mustered a total of 262 officers. These received higher pay when serving overseas and were consulted only when strictly needed, for example to conduct siege operations or to build military infrastructures like bridges. The labour force for the Royal Engineers was provided by the Royal Military Artificers (known as the Royal Military Artificers and Labourers until 1798), a small technical corps consisting of twelve companies of military workers, each commanded by a sub-lieutenant and a staff sergeant. The Royal Military Artificers performed a series of

Soldier of the Royal Artillery with M1797 dress.

auxiliary tasks that were absolutely fundamental for the life of the British Army in the field, which included building and carpentry. During the Napoleonic Wars, the dozen companies of the corps were scattered across the British Empire as follows: eight in Britain, two in Gibraltar, one in the West Indies and one in Canada (Nova Scotia). The artificers of the British Army were organized as an independent military branch of service only in 1772; until that time, their tasks had been performed by unreliable civilian workers who were contracted according to circumstances. In 1787, the corps was expanded and assumed the new official denomination of Royal Military Artificers and Labourers. During the first phase of the Napoleonic Wars, these mostly served in small detachments, since their companies were usually broken up and dispersed on the various fronts. Wellington was always critical of his artificers, and thus he decided to reorganize them in 1812. They then assumed the new official denomination of Royal Sappers and Miners and their numbers were expanded to 2,800 men. They were now to be commanded by the commissioned officers of the Royal Engineers; in addition, they no longer served in small detachments but in companies. After being retrained in Britain, 300 workers of the Royal Sappers and Miners served with distinction in the Iberian Peninsula during 1813. In 1815, they made a significant contribution to the British military effort that culminated in the Battle of Waterloo. During the Belgian campaign, each division of Wellington's army had an attached brigade (company) of sappers and miners. Each company transported its own working tools and entrenching tools for at least 500 infantrymen. Until the reorganization of 1812, the military workers of the British Army did not have their own wagons for transporting materials, and thus were dependent on the artillery for such movement. For the Belgian campaign of 1815, the Royal Sappers and Miners deployed 550 drivers, 160 wagons and 1,000 draught horses. It should be noted, however, that only some of the drivers were 'militarized' ones from the Corps of Royal Artillery Drivers.

In addition to the Royal Engineers and the Royal Sappers and Miners, the British Army comprised another technical corps of military engineers: the Royal Staff Corps. This was organized in 1798 and was required to provide engineer service under the direct control of the British Army's Commander-in-Chief. In practice, differently from the Royal Engineers and Royal Sappers – who were scattered in small detachments across the British Empire – the Royal Staff Corps was to act as the unified engineer force of the British Army's General Staff. Initially, it consisted of just four companies, but was later expanded to become a battalion. Its officers had much in common with the Royal Engineers and were usually employed singlely; the rankers, however, performed the same functions as the Royal Sappers and Miners. Each company of the Royal Staff Corps included a sergeant major and a quartermaster

Officer of the Royal Artillery with M1797 uniform.

sergeant; its rankers were all paid more than the ordinary infantrymen of the British Army and thus enjoyed an elite status compared with the Royal Sappers. The Royal Staff Corps was finally disbanded in 1837, its members being absorbed into the Royal Engineers and Royal Sappers.

In addition to the Corps of Royal Artillery Drivers, the British Army also had a Royal Waggon Train that was tasked with transporting all those materials of the army that did not belong to the artillery. This was organized in 1798, mostly with men drafted from the cavalry, and initially consisted of just three troops. Each of these troops comprised the following elements: three sergeants, three corporals, one trumpeter, three artificers and sixty-two privates. During the Napoleonic Wars, the Royal Waggon Train was progressively expanded and, by 1814, it was structured on fourteen troops with around 1,900 men. Generally speaking, like their equivalents in the Royal Artillery, the drivers of the Royal Waggon Train were not noted for their discipline and efficiency.

Among the technical corps of the British Army that took part to the Napoleonic Wars, we should also mention the Staff Corps of Cavalry, which was the first military police unit ever formed in Britain. While operating in the Iberian Peninsula, Wellington understood that it was absolutely vital to organize a provost corps that could enforce discipline among the British soldiers who operated in Spain and Portugal. At that time, it was important to preserve the rights of the local populations from the frequent 'irregularities' committed by the British soldiers. As a result, in 1813, four troops of mounted military policemen were organized and became known as the Staff Corps of Cavalry. Two of these were with Wellington's army in Spain, one was raised in England and another in Ireland. The members of the two troops deployed in the Iberian Peninsula were all volunteers from the cavalry regiments who had a sound personal reputation. They comprised the following elements: four captains, four lieutenants, two cornets, six sergeants, six corporals and 120 troopers. The new military policemen were intended to prevent desertion and looting, but were also tasked with other auxiliary duties. They received an extra pay for their services and wore a distinctive uniform. In 1814, the Staff Corps of Cavalry was disbanded when the British Army left the Iberian Peninsula. During the following year, however, it was temporarily re-formed on two troops and took part in the Belgian campaign before being disbanded again in 1818.

Uniforms and equipment

Generally speaking, the uniforms of the Royal Artillery and the smaller technical corps were very similar to those of the British line infantry or light cavalry: the Foot Artillery, Royal Engineers, Royal Sappers and Royal Staff Corps were dressed similarly to the line infantry, while the uniforms of the Horse Artillery, Rocket Troops, Royal Artillery Drivers and Royal Waggon Train were very like the light cavalry. In 1793, the Foot Artillery had long-tailed coats, which were worn open from the neck and sloped away at the waist. The main colour of this item of dress was dark blue (the distinctive colour of the Royal Artillery), with collar and cuffs in red. The lapels on the front of the coat were also red, while the turn-backs were white. The skirt and linings over which the coat was worn were white. The dark blue coat had horizontal pockets and could be worn with the lapels buttoned over or folded back. All the buttonholes of the coat (on collar, cuffs and frontal lapels) had some additional yellow lace. The headgear was a black bicorn with yellow external edging, black cockade and white plume. In 1796, the model of coat, which had not changed since the days of the American Revolution, was modified in order to be more practical and up to date: it was fastened to the waist, while the lapels were retained (for the moment) but were made to button over on every occasion. The collar was modified too: now it was a standing one, instead of lying flat. In October 1797, the lapels were officially abolished for all non-officers, and thus the dark blue coat of the British Foot Artillery became a single-breasted jacket. This no longer had tails (which were replaced by 'false' tails), and started to have vertical pockets on the back. On the front, the new jacket had a single line of buttons and was decorated with yellow lace embroidered under the buttons and on the buttonholes. The main colour of the uniform remained dark blue, but collar and round cuffs were red, piped in yellow. The jacket had red shoulder straps piped in yellow; these had been present on the pre-1796 uniform, but now they received a yellow crest where they were sewn to the shoulder and were pointed at the other end (where they were secured, close to the collar, by a small button). With the new uniform, grey trousers were worn during winter and white ones in the summer. In 1800, the bicorn was replaced by the shako as the headgear of the Foot Artillery. The M1800 shako was commonly known as the stovepipe shako because of its distinctive shape; its introduction was very innovative at the time, since the British Army was one of the first in the world to adopt the shako as standard headgear. It was made of lacquered leather and had a flat peak on the front, while the crown had a cylindrical shape which resembled that of a stovepipe. On the top of the crown was a worsted wool tuft in white, at the base of which there was a black cockade with a small button at its centre. The front of the

Soldier of the Royal Artillery with M1797 dress and stovepipe shako.

shako had a large plate made of thin brass, with a specific design die-stamped on the rear that reproduced the Royal Artillery's coat of arms.

In 1812, a new model of shako was introduced, which was more comfortable and more practical to wear on the battlefield. This later became known as the Belgian or Waterloo shako, since it was first used on a large scale during the Belgian campaign of 1815. The main feature of this new headgear was that it had a crown that sloped down at the back, producing a false front. On the rear, the crown was also a little broader. Like the previous shako, it was made of black felt. The false front was edged with black lace, and on the front of the headgear there was a peak made of lacquered leather. The M1812 shako had a white worsted tuft on the left side, at the base of which there was the usual black cockade, held in place by a button. On the front of the shako there was a yellow twist cord with a tassel at each end; a doubled loop knot was formed to shorten the cord into two lengths of chain, with an un-knotted length at the centre. The cord was worn with the doubled loop end hooked behind the cockade, with the two lengths of loop knots either side of the shako plate and the two tassels on the right. The frontal plate of the M1812 shako was made of brass and reproduced a design that was specific to the Royal Artillery.

Until 1797, the officers of the Foot Artillery were dressed very much like their men, but with some differences: the external edging of their bicorn was golden, they had golden epaulettes on the shoulders and wore a red sash around the waist. With the adoption of the new M1797 dress, the officers of the Foot Artillery started to be uniformed as follows: black bicorn with white plume and black cockade, dark blue double-breasted tunic with red standing collar and round cuffs, golden epaulettes showing rank on the shoulders, red sash worn around the waist, white trousers and black leather boots. Belt equipment was white leather both for officers and rankers. Until 1797, the officers of the Royal Engineers were dressed like those of the Foot Artillery, but the facing colour of their uniform was black instead of red, while they did not have additional yellow lace on the buttonholes of their tunic. The new uniform adopted from 1797 was as follows: black bicorn with white plume and black cockade, dark blue double-breasted tunic with black standing collar and round cuffs, golden epaulettes showing rank on the shoulders, red sash worn around the waist, white trousers and black leather boots. Until 1797, the Royal Military Artificers wore the following dress: black round hat with yellow bottom band and red plume applied over a black cockade, dark blue long-tailed coat with black standing collar and round cuffs, black frontal lapels, additional yellow lace on the buttonholes of the coat (on collar, cuffs and lapels), white waistcoat and trousers, and white leather belt equipment. On active service, the plume of the hat and the frontal lapels of the coat were usually removed. In 1797, the following new uniform came into use for the

Soldier of the Royal Artillery with M1797 uniform and Belgian shako.

Royal Military Artificers: black stovepipe shako with white plume, black cockade and brass frontal plate, dark blue single-breasted jacket with black standing collar piped in yellow and black round cuffs, black shoulder straps piped in yellow, additional yellow lace on the buttonholes of the jacket (on the front and on the cuffs), white trousers and black gaiters. When the Royal Military Artificers were reorganized as the Royal Sappers and Miners in 1812, they received the following new uniform: black Belgian shako with white plume, yellow cords, black cockade and brass frontal plate, red single-breasted jacket with dark blue standing collar piped in yellow and dark blue round cuffs, dark blue shoulder straps piped in yellow, additional yellow lace on the buttonholes of the jacket (on the front and on the cuffs), grey trousers and black gaiters. On active service a simpler version of the jacket was worn, which did not have additional yellow lace on the buttonholes and piping to the collar and shoulder straps. An undress cap made of black leather was also used, which had the brass initials 'RS & M' on the front. In 1812, following their integration with the Royal Sappers and Miners, the Royal Engineers also received a new red uniform: black bicorn with white plume and black cockade, red double-breasted tunic with dark blue standing collar and round cuffs, additional golden lace on the buttonholes of the collar and cuffs, golden epaulettes showing rank on the shoulders, red sash worn around the waist, grey trousers with red side-stripe and black leather boots. The soldiers of the Royal Staff Corps were dressed as follows after 1800: black shako with brass frontal plate, black cockade and white-and-red plume, red single-breasted jacket with dark blue standing collar and round cuffs, white piping to collar and cuffs, dark blue shoulder straps piped in white, dark blue trousers, black leather short boots and white leather belt equipment.

Until 1799, the troopers of the Horse Artillery were dressed very similarly to the Light Dragoons, but the piping colour of their uniform was yellow rather than white. Their uniform comprised the following: black leather Tarleton helmet with black peak, black fur crest, white plume (worn on the left side), black band with yellow stripes wrapped around the bottom part, black cockade on the back, brass chinscale and brass unit badge representing a flaming grenade (worn on the right side); dark blue sleeveless shell jacket with red collar piped in yellow, yellow frontal frogging and yellow piping to the front and bottom edges; dark blue short-tailed sleeved waistcoat with red pointed cuffs piped in yellow, red shoulder straps piped in yellow and additional yellow braiding on the buttonholes of the waistcoat's front; white trousers, black leather boots and white belt equipment. In 1799, the following new Horse Artillery uniform was introduced, which was retained in service until the end of the Napoleonic Wars: black leather Tarleton helmet with black peak, black fur crest, white plume (worn on the left side), black band with yellow stripes wrapped around

Officer of the Horse Artillery with M1793 dress.

the bottom part, brass chinscale and brass unit badge representing a flaming grenade (worn on the right side); dark blue dolman with red collar and pointed cuffs piped in yellow, yellow piping to the bottom edge and the rear seams, and yellow frontal frogging with three vertical rows of buttons; grey trousers with red side-stripe and brown leather internal reinforcement, black leather short boots and white leather belt equipment. The Rocket Troops, organized in 1813, were uniformed exactly like the Horse Artillery, of which they were part. The Royal Artillery Drivers were initially dressed with a very simple uniform, of clear civilian cut: black leather undress cap with the brass initials 'C R A D' on the front, dark blue single-breasted jacket with red collar and round cuffs, and three rows of vertical buttons on the front, white trousers and black leather boots. Around 1811, this uniform was progressively substituted by a new dress, which was as follows: black leather Tarleton helmet with black peak, black fur crest, white plume (worn on the left side), dark blue band with yellow stripes wrapped around the bottom part, brass chinscale and brass unit badge representing the shield of the Artillery Ordnance (worn on the right side); dark blue single-breasted jacket with three vertical rows of buttons on the front, having double yellow piping, red collar and pointed cuffs piped in yellow; grey trousers with red side-stripe and brown leather internal reinforcement, black leather short boots and white leather belt equipment. Until 1811, the Royal Waggon Train wore the same uniform as the Royal Artillery Drivers, but with different brass initials on the black leather undress cap. In 1811, the following new dress was adopted by them, which was similar to that worn by the Royal Artillery Drivers but was red instead of dark blue and had a different headgear: black shako with white top band, white pompom, white-and-red short plume, white cords, black leather peak, white metal chinscale and black cockade with white external edge; red single-breasted jacket with three vertical rows of buttons on the front having double white piping, dark blue collar and pointed cuffs piped in white; grey trousers with dark blue side-stripe and brown leather internal reinforcement, black leather short boots and white leather belt equipment. Initially, the members of the Staff Corps of Cavalry retained the uniforms of their former regiments and simply wore a red scarf tied around their right shoulder as a mark of distinction. However, they soon received a red uniform that was very similar to that worn by the Light Dragoons: black shako with white top band, white pompom, red short plume, white cords, black leather peak, white metal chinscale and black cockade with white external edge; red tunic with dark blue collar and pointed cuffs piped in white, dark blue frontal plastron piped in white, dark blue shoulder straps piped in white, white piping to the rear seams of the tunic, dark blue short turnbacks and red pockets piped in dark blue on the back of the turnbacks; red-and-dark-blue sash wrapped around the waist; grey trousers with dark blue double side-stripe, black leather short boots, black leather sabretache and white leather belt equipment.

Chapter 5

Yeomanry, Fencible and Foreign Units

When hostilities between Great Britain and Revolutionary France began in 1792, many local communities living on the southern coast of England started to send an increasing number of written petitions to the government. Fearing that the French could land on their territory, the inhabitants of southern Britain required weapons and equipment from the government so that they could organize local military units made up of volunteers. Initially, the government was not interested in the possibility of forming volunteer corps across Britain, mostly because it feared that the ideals of the French Revolution could be transferred to England and thereby transform the armed volunteers into a potential menace for internal stability. In 1794, however, it became clear that the new volunteer units would be controlled by the local aristocracy, and thus the government decided to promulgate the Volunteer Act. This permitted the formation of a new military organization: the Volunteer Corps. This would be made up of volunteer units that would be raised and maintained thanks to the subscriptions of wealthy local donors (most of whom were aristocrats). The members of the Volunteer Corps were tasked with three main duties: garrisoning the coastal batteries of southern England, patrolling the countryside in search of enemy spies or political agitators, and supporting the regular soldiers in case of a large-scale enemy invasion.

The cavalry of the Volunteer Corps was known as the Yeomanry and consisted of individuals from the propertied social classes who were rich enough to maintain a good horse and the necessary cavalry equipment. The officers were usually members of the gentry, who enlisted in the Yeomanry with the hope of kick-starting a brilliant political or military career. After the implementation of the Volunteer Act, dozens of volunteer units were raised across Britain, although it soon became apparent that there were insufficient cavalry units. Since the British government was convinced that local light cavalry would play a crucial part in repulsing any French invasion, in 1796 it passed the Provisional Cavalry Act. Under the act, a new military organization known as Provisional Cavalry was to be formed. This was organized at county level, with each county given a quota of provisional cavalrymen that it was expected to provide. Each horse owner of Britain was to provide one trooper for every ten horses owned, while those who owned fewer than ten horses were collected into groups which were each required to provide one man. The Provisional Cavalry

Act of 1796 was very unpopular because it was based on strict obligations; as a result, the quality of the recruits provided for the new Provisional Cavalry was quite low. While members of the Yeomanry cavalry were paid for their military services when mobilized, members of the Provisional Cavalry received a regular wage. In 1798, understanding that the Provisional Cavalry Act had been a failure, the government exempted from the obligation of raising provisional cavalrymen all those counties where at least 75 per cent of the demanded quota of Provisional Cavalry was filled by the local Yeomanry. As a result, when the infantry of the Volunteer Corps and the Provisional Cavalry were disbanded in 1802, the Yeomanry was retained in service, continuing right through to 1908, when it was absorbed into the newly organized Territorial Force. In total, only seven regiments of Provisional Cavalry were ever embodied, and only one of them saw combat action, during the Irish Rebellion of

Soldier of the Horse Artillery with M1793 uniform.

1798. The Yeomanry, however, performed a series of important auxiliary duties for the duration of the Napoleonic Wars, and on several occasions it was employed to crush local rebellions and riots.

Today, neither the Volunteer Corps nor the Provisional Cavalry are very well known, but it should be noted that it was only thanks to them that no conscription law had to be enacted in Britain during the Napoleonic Period. These two military organizations provided a large number of 'paramilitary' auxiliaries for several years, and thus contributed to the British war effort in a significant way.

Unlike the Yeomanry and the Provincial Cavalry, the Fencible Regiments were a category of regular troops that performed some important auxiliary duties for the British Army. The term 'Fencibles' derives from the word 'defensible', since these were static units formed specifically for the defence of a certain territory. They were fixed garrison corps, similar to the units of the militia: since they were recruited on a local basis, they had strong links with their home territory, albeit being part of the regular British military. Generally speaking, the Fencible Regiments were temporary units, which were raised for active service only when Britain was under threat of foreign invasion. They were made up of volunteers but were commanded by officers from the regular army. With the outbreak of hostilities with Revolutionary France, there was a strong possibility that a French invasion could take place in southern England, and thus many Fencible units were raised on British soil. These proved to be of great use during the Irish Rebellion of 1798, when a small French expeditionary corps disembarked in Ireland to support the local insurgents. When it became apparent that the rebellion in Ireland had been crushed and that a French invasion of England would never happen, most of the Fencible Regiments were disbanded (especially after the signing of the Peace of Amiens between Britain and France in 1802). The following mounted Fencible Regiments were active in Great Britain from 1793–1800:

- First Regiment of British Fencible Cavalry
- Ancient British Regiment
- Ayrshire Regiment
- Berwickshire Corps
- Cambridgeshire Regiment
- Cinque Ports Regiment
- Cornwall Regiment
- Dumfriesshire Regiment
- East and West Lothian Regiment
- Fifeshire Corps

- Hampshire Regiment
- Lanark and Dunbarton Regiment
- Lancashire Regiment
- Loyal Essex Regiment
- Mid Lothian Regiment
- New Romney Regiment
- Norfolk Regiment
- Oxfordshire Regiment
- Pembrokeshire Corps
- Perthshire Regiment
- Princess Royal's Own Regiment
- Princess of Wales' Regiment
- Roxbrough and Selkirkshire Regiment
- Rutland Regiment
- Somersetshire Regiment
- Surrey Regiment
- Sussex Regiment
- Warwickshire Regiment
- Windsor Foresters
- First Regiment of Irish Fencible Cavalry
- Second Regiment of Irish Fencible Cavalry

Each of these regiments was commanded by a staff that comprised eighteen commissioned officers from the regular British Army and was structured on a variable number of troops, each of which comprised a total of eighty privates. In the early months of 1800, all the cavalry units of the Fencibles were rapidly disbanded.

At the outbreak of the Revolutionary Wars, the British Army comprised a single unit made up of foreign professional soldiers, the 60th Regiment of Foot. With the expansion of the military operations conducted against France, however, Britain was obliged to raise a large number of mercenary corps from foreign sources in order to augment the numbers of the regular forces and to have those kinds of troops that were absent or scarce in the British Army (most notably light infantry and light cavalry). During the period from 1793–1802, these were mostly made up of French Royalists, who had been forced to abandon their country after the execution of Louis XVI and who were collectively known as *émigrés*. During late 1794, the French Republic invaded the Netherlands and transformed it into a puppet Batavian Republic, whereupon a large number of Dutch soldiers became available for British service as foreign mercenaries. Several units of 'strangers' were also raised from Germany and

Officer of the Horse Artillery with M1799 dress.

Soldier of the Horse Artillery with M1799 uniform.

Switzerland, two areas of Europe that had always exported mercenaries and could contribute expert light corps to the British cause. In 1802, with the Peace of Amiens, most of the 'first generation' of foreign corps described above were disbanded. During the following years, however, several new foreign units were raised by the British Army on the new fronts where it began to be involved. What follows is a brief overview of the foreign cavalry and artillery units that served under the British flag between 1800 and 1815:

York Hussars: Raised in 1793, this unit was mostly made up of German soldiers and consisted of three squadrons with two companies each (for a total of 600 men). After taking part in the Flanders Campaign, the York Hussars were sent to Haiti, where they suffered heavy casualties. Before returning to Britain in 1799, the unit absorbed several foreigners who had been part of recently disbanded cavalry corps. The York Hussars were disbanded in July 1802.

Hompesch's Mounted Rifles: Raised by Charles de Hompesch in Germany during 1796, this unit consisted of four troops with 114 men in each. It took part in the military operations against the 1798 Irish Rebellion and in the Egyptian campaign. The corps was disbanded in September 1802.

King's Dutch Brigade: In 1795, following the fall of the Dutch Republic, the *stadtholter* William V fled to Britain together with his son, Frederick of Orange-Nassau. Frederick was a capable military commander and soon started planning the organization of a Dutch Army in exile. This was raised from the many Dutch troops who had abandoned their home country and entered Prussian territory in order to avoid capture. In 1795, Prussia was a neutral country. Frederick's loyal soldiers moved to Hanover and were later transferred to Britain, where some of them were absorbed into foreign units serving in the British Army. During the 1799 Netherlands campaign, which ended in failure, the British captured several soldiers of the Batavian Republic; these included many deserters and mutineers, who were united with the Dutch soldiers already in Britain to form a large and independent Dutch military corps. This was known as the King's Dutch Brigade and was organized on the following units: four regiments of line infantry with eighteen companies each, one regiment of jagers (riflemen) with eighteen companies, one battalion of artillery with six companies and a small engineer corps with one company of pioneers. The Dutch Brigade, comprising 5,000 soldiers, was commanded by Frederick of Orange-Nassau. In November 1800, the engineers/pioneers were absorbed into the artillery and a second artillery battalion with four companies was created; in addition, the two light companies of each line infantry regiment were detached to create two new jager battalions with four companies each. In 1802, due to the Peace of Amiens, the Dutch Brigade was disbanded without having seen action.

Malta Coast Artillery: This little corps consisted of two companies that were charged with manning the coastal batteries of Malta. It was formed from local militiamen in 1800 after the British reoccupied the island.

Maltese Military Artificers: This was also a small auxiliary corps made up of Maltese soldiers. It consisted of two companies, raised in 1806.

Maltese Police Corps: This small paramilitary corps comprised around 200 men who acted as a sort of gendarmerie for the island of Malta.

Minorca Light Dragoons: A short-lived light cavalry company was raised from some Hungarians during the British occupation of Minorca. It was disbanded in 1802 after less than two years of service.

Foreign Hussars: Formed during 1810 in Sicily, the Foreign Hussars assembled together all the soldiers of the foreign units in British service on the island who could ride a horse. They consisted of a single troop that was attached to the 20th Light Dragoons and was deployed in the Iberian Peninsula until being disbanded in 1813.

Among the foreign troops at the service of Britain during the Napoleonic Wars, the King's German Legion or KGL was without doubt the largest and best of them all. It was a miniature army comprising military units of every kind and fought with great valour during most of Wellington's campaign. The German soldiers of the KGL were considered to be the best professionals of the British Army, together with the members of a few other elite corps. The German state of Hanover was in personal union with the Kingdom of Great Britain from the early eighteenth century, and thus the two countries were ruled by the same monarch. In practice, however, they had different institutions and were governed as two autonomous states; Hanover, for example, had its own army and its own administration. Nevertheless, during the various European conflicts of the eighteenth century, Hanover always fought on Britain's side. Bordering with France, it was particularly exposed to foreign invasion and on several occasions had to count on British military support in order to preserve its territorial integrity. Among the military forces of the German states, the Hanoverian Army was one of the most efficient and professional. At the outbreak of the Revolutionary Wars, it comprised the following units:

Soldiers of the Rocket Troops (left) and the Horse Artillery (right), both wearing M1799 dress.

- One regiment of Guard infantry, on two battalions with six companies each (one of grenadiers, five of musketeers), plus an artillery section with four guns
- Fifteen regiments of line infantry, on two battalions with six companies each (one of grenadiers, five of musketeers), plus an artillery section with four guns
- One regiment of Guard cavalry, on four squadrons with two companies each
- Four regiments of heavy cavalry, on four squadrons with two companies each
- Four regiments of dragoons, on four squadrons with two companies each
- Two regiments of light dragoons, on four squadrons with two companies each

- One regiment of artillery, on two battalions with five companies each
- One Miner and Sapper Company
- One Pontoon and Pioneer Company

In 1803, after hostilities resumed between Britain and France, Hanover was invaded within a few days by Napoleon's forces. Isolated and surrounded by hostile territories, it

Soldier of the Rocket Troops with M1799 uniform.

was practically impossible to defend. The Hanoverian Army was formally disbanded, but thousands of its members were willing to continue the fight against France under the flags of their royal family. Consequently, in August 1803, the British government issued a proclamation that invited all the former members of the Hanoverian Army to join the ranks of the British military. The German volunteers were to be assembled into a new corps known as The King's Germans, which would preserve the traditions of the Hanoverian Army. During the following weeks, hundreds of volunteers responded to the call and started to leave Germany. Most of them were embarked in the port of Husum on the North Sea and travelled to England within a few days. The German volunteers were so numerous that it soon became clear that a new fighting force comprising all arms could be formed. The depot of the new corps was initially placed on the Isle of Wight, but it had to be transferred to Portsmouth because of the increasingly large number of recruits coming from Hanover. By December 1803, the new unit of the British Army had received its official denomination of the King's German Legion. During 1804, the KGL continued to expand thanks to the arrival of new volunteers, and thus by the middle of 1805 it comprised the following units:

- Four battalions of line infantry
- Two battalions of light infantry
- One regiment of dragoons
- Two regiments of light dragoons
- Three companies (batteries) of foot artillery
- Two companies (batteries) of horse artillery
- Engineer Corps (made up of a few specialized officers)

The internal organization of these units was almost the same as their British equivalents. Their officers were mostly German and the discipline of the rankers was excellent. During the War of the Third Coalition in 1805, while Napoleon was fighting against the Austrians and Russians in Central Europe, Britain assembled an expeditionary force with the objective of reconquering Hanover. This comprised 6,000 soldiers from the KGL and was able to occupy Hanover practically without fighting, as the French were heavily involved on other fronts. When Napoleon triumphed at Austerlitz, however, the situation changed and the British expeditionary force was forced to leave Germany in order to avoid a direct confrontation with the bulk of the French Army. Yet the few months spent in Hanover had very positive consequences for the KGL, as thousands of local volunteers decided to join the legion and followed it back to Britain. Thanks to the new recruits, it was possible to organize the following additional corps:

- Four battalions of line infantry
- One regiment of dragoons
- One regiment of light dragoons
- One company (battery) of foot artillery

In 1807, the KGL was sent to Denmark as part of the British force that attacked Copenhagen. The following year, it was transported to the Iberian Peninsula, where it would remain until 1814. In Spain, the German soldiers in the British Army took part in all the most decisive battles fought against the French, and on several occasions it was their great courage that determined the outcome of a clash. Wellington, who commanded these men for many years, considered them as the best of his troops. The soldiers of the KGL were able to endure any kind of hardships, and despite suffering heavy losses they always retained a high morale. The five cavalry regiments – two of dragoons and three of light dragoons – had four squadrons each; a single squadron consisted of two troops and each of the latter comprised the following elements: one captain, one lieutenant, one cornet, one quartermaster sergeant (sergeant major from 1809), four sergeants, four corporals, one trumpeter and seventy-six troopers. In 1812, one squadron was added to each regiment, but this organizational change lasted only until early 1815. During 1813, the two dragoon regiments were converted into light dragoon units, with the three regiments of light dragoons becoming hussar units. Each artillery company/battery (on foot or mounted) consisted of one captain, one second captain, four lieutenants and 219 NCOs/soldiers. Each battery had four guns and two howitzers: the guns could be 6-pdrs, 9-pdrs or 12-pdrs, while the howitzers could be of 5.5in or 8in calibre.

In 1815, after having participated in the occupation of southern France, the KGL fought its last campaign in Belgium. The corps had already been transferred to Flanders when the hostilities with France resumed, but its destiny had not yet been decided: Hanover had been freed by the French and was now rebuilding its national army, so it would have been obvious to use the KGL as the main core around which to re-form the Hanoverian Army. Wellington, however, was against this plan and wanted to keep the veterans of the KGL under his orders as part of the British Army. During the few months of Napoleon's first exile, the internal strength of the KGL units was greatly reduced, but no corps was disbanded. The companies in each infantry battalion were reduced from ten to six, while the troops in each cavalry regiment were cut from eight to six. The 7,000 remaining soldiers of the corps participated in the Battle of Waterloo and, as usual, fought with great distinction. In particular, they defended the key position of La Haye Sainte to the last man, their actions helping enable Wellington to win the battle. By December 1815, with the Napoleonic Wars

Soldiers (left and right) and NCO (centre) of the Royal Military Artificers wearing pre-1797 parade dress.

over for several months, the KGL was finally ordered to march home to Hanover. Subsequently, all the units of the corps were disbanded during early 1816. Most of the officers and men who had served under Wellington for so many years decided to enlist in the new Hanoverian Army, which was still in the process of being reorganized. The many battle honours of the glorious KGL were inherited by the new Hanoverian units, which acquired a great amount of competence and experience thanks to the inclusion of the KGL veterans. With the soldiers coming from the disbanded KGL, the new Hanoverian Army of 1815 was structured as follows:

- Nine battalions of line infantry
- One battalion of light infantry
- Thirty battalions of militia infantry
- Three regiments of hussars
- Three companies (batteries) of foot artillery

Soldier (left) and NCO (right) of the Royal Military Artificers wearing pre-1797 campaign uniform.

Chapter 6

Colonial Cavalry and Artillery

Canada

When the USA gained its independence in 1783, Britain was able to retain possession of Canada, which remained as the largest colony of the British Crown, at a time when India was still administered by the private East India Company and Australia was just in the early phases of colonization. From an administrative point of view, British Canada was divided as follows: Lower Canada, Upper Canada, Nova Scotia, New Brunswick, Newfoundland, Prince Edward Island and Cape Breton Island. The economies of all these territories had a precise role in the global commercial system created by Britain, and were mostly based on the fur trade and fishing. Exploitation of forests for wood was also a very important activity: during the long wars against Revolutionary and Napoleonic France, Canada became extremely important for Britain as a source of high-quality wood for building warships. In general, the territory of Canada was not economically developed like that of the USA, but its population (albeit being quite small) was made up of sturdy and courageous people. The troops garrisoning Canada between 1800 and 1815 were of three different kinds: British regular units, Canadian militia units and Canadian volunteer units. The militia system of Canada derived from the French colonial period and remained extremely efficient under the British, as the US Army learned during its attempted invasion of Canada. In 1812, at the outbreak of war with the USA, the British regular military units stationed in Canada were extremely limited, consisting of just 6,034 men and including the following corps:

- 8th Regiment of Foot
- 41st Regiment of Foot
- 49th Regiment of Foot
- 100th Regiment of Foot
- Six companies of the 98th Regiment of Foot
- Four companies of the 99th Regiment of Foot
- 10th Royal Veteran Battalion
- Detachments of the Royal Artillery
- Detachments of the Royal Engineers

- Detachments of the Royal Military Artificers/Royal Sappers and Miners
- Canadian Fencible Infantry
- Nova Scotia Fencible Infantry
- New Brunswick Fencible Infantry
- Newfoundland Fencible Infantry

There was no cavalry, while the artillery/technical corps were present only with small detachments comprising just a few men. In Canada, like in the USA, the militia was formed by all the able-bodied men who were eligible for military service according to their age. Since the foundation of the first French settlements in the early seventeenth century, the Canadians had to adopt a form of local military organization in order to repulse the violent raids of the various native tribes. This system was implemented during the eighteenth century and saw the Canadian militiamen fighting with great valour against the British and their native allies during the French-Indian War. Unlike what happened in the Thirteen Colonies, the militia units of French Canada were under quite strict control from the central authorities of the colony. Generally speaking the Canadian militias had fewer men than their American equivalents, but their members had superior military capabilities. Most of the settlers living in Canada were huntsmen, and so were used to travelling long distances in the worst weather conditions. They had a deep knowledge of the vast forests and plains surrounding them, and were all excellent marksmen (employing long and rifled muskets exactly like the American colonists). Thanks to their high mobility and great capacity to organize ambushes, the Canadian militiamen were able to fight against the natives on almost equal terms: they had a skilled knowledge of guerrilla warfare and could launch surprise attacks very easily. The militiamen of Canada, in addition, were ready to operate during winter and had all the necessary equipment to survive extremely cold temperatures. Rivers and lakes were no barriers for them, since their use of canoes was extremely common. In general, albeit being quite few compared with their American opponents, the Canadian militiamen were excellent soldiers.

The British inherited the militia system from the French and did nothing to change it, although they did try to regularize as much as possible the Canadian militia units to transform them into a proper auxiliary army that could support the regular forces. Most of Canada's population consisted of Francophone settlers, who had always been extremely loyal to France until the very last days of the French-Indian War. Consequently, at the outbreak of the War of 1812, the British authorities feared that these men could refuse to serve in the militia or revolt against the Crown. Yet the Canadian colonists all remained loyal to Britain, Francophones and Anglophones alike. The Canadians already considered their territories to be a nation, so the foreign

NCO (left) and soldiers (right) of the Royal Military Artificers wearing M1797 parade dress.

aggression of the USA did nothing but augment their patriotic feelings. From 1791, administratively, the territory of Canada was divided into two provinces: Lower Canada and Upper Canada. There was also the Indian Territory and the smaller Atlantic Colonies, the former comprising all the unsettled lands that were located west of the Great Lakes, while the latter were formed by the smaller British colonies situated on the Atlantic coast (Nova Scotia, New Brunswick, Newfoundland, Prince Edward Island and Cape Breton Island). For each of these territories, we will now list the cavalry and artillery units that were active there.

Lower Canada: This province, corresponding to the former territory of New France, comprised most of the Francophone settlers in British-held North America. It had a much larger population than Upper Canada and included the three most important cities in Canada: Quebec, Montreal and Trois-Rivières. The militia of this colony (which had originally been established by the French in the mid-seventeenth century) comprised an active force (known as the Select Militia) and a reserve one (the Sedentary Militia). The former was activated only in case of foreign menace and consisted of the best elements from the Sedentary Militia. When a unit was called to serve, no matter if coming from the Select or Sedentary Militia, it received the further title of 'Embodied' (which meant it was attached to the regulars). Until the outbreak of hostilities with the USA, the militia of Lower Canada did not include any unit of cavalry or artillery, but the following ones were raised during the conflict:

- **Compagnie des Guides:** This was a small cavalry unit, also known as the Corps of Guides. Formed in September 1812, it comprised just two officers and thirty troopers.
- **Canadian Light Dragoons:** Recruited in the Montreal district during the spring of 1813, this was a small cavalry corps of just eighty men (assembled into a single troop). The unit saw much action and took part in several engagements, being finally disbanded only in May 1815.
- **Dorchester Provincial Light Dragoons:** Raised during the spring of 1813 like the Canadian Light Dragoons, this corps was another small cavalry unit. It consisted of a single troop with sixty-eight men, who were armed and equipped by the government but had to buy horses and uniforms at their own expense. The Dorchester Provincial Light Dragoons served in Quebec until being disbanded in March 1815.
- **Royal Militia Artillery:** This unit consisted of just one officer and twenty-two gunners, who were detached from the urban militia of Montreal in September 1812 in order to be absorbed into the Select Embodied Militia.
- **Corps of Provincial Royal Artillery Drivers:** Formed in April 1813, this small corps was attached to the regular detachments of the Royal Artillery that operated in the Montreal district. The Canadians had to provide drivers for the batteries of the regular artillery, since most of the British artillerymen were employed as gunners and not for auxiliary duties.

When it was directly menaced by the American invasion, Lower Canada also mobilized its Sedentary Militia. This numbered some 54,000 militiamen, who were organized in two different ways according to their ethnic origins. The Sedentary Militia of the Francophone communities had the parish company as its basic unit, while that of the Anglophone settlers was organized according to counties in traditional British style. In addition, in the major urban centres of Quebec, Montreal and Trois-Rivières there were several autonomous urban militias, which comprised some cavalry and artillery corps. The urban militias of Quebec and Montreal each deployed one troop of cavalry and two companies of artillery, which were all formed from well-educated gentlemen/volunteers. These took part in no significant military actions during the War of 1812 and were disbanded as soon as the American threat ended in 1815.

Officer of the Royal Engineers with M1812 uniform.

Upper Canada: This province had initially been mostly inhabited by Loyalist Americans who abandoned the Thirteen Colonies during the Revolution against Britain. Much of the combat operations of the 1812–1815 war took place on its territory, and thus it suffered greatly from the devastations caused by the battling armies. Despite having a smaller population than Lower Canada, the province of Upper Canada made a significant contribution to the British war effort. Geographically, Upper Canada comprised the vast territory located between the western border of Quebec province and the city of Windsor on Lake Huron. In total, the province comprised eight districts divided into several counties. The Sedentary Militia of Upper Canada was much younger than that of Lower Canada, having been organized for the first time in 1793. Similarly to what happened among the Anglophone communities of Lower Canada, it was based on the county unit. Until the outbreak of hostilities with the USA, the militia of Upper Canada did not include any unit of cavalry or artillery, but during the conflict the following units were raised:

- **Provincial Light Dragoons:** These consisted of just three small corps, each formed in a different county of Upper Canada. The Niagara Provincial Light Dragoons were a troop of just fifty men, which was renamed as the Niagara Frontier Guides on 24 October 1814. The other two troops were created in April 1813 and later assembled into a single unit.
- **Incorporated Artillery Company:** Raised in March 1813, it comprised both artillerymen and artillery drivers who were absorbed into the Select Embodied Militia.
- **Provincial Royal Artillery Drivers:** Formed in January 1813, this small corps (just two companies) was attached to the regular detachments of the Royal Artillery that were operating in Upper Canada. The local Canadians had to provide drivers for the batteries of the regular artillery, since most of the British artillerymen were employed as gunners and not for auxiliary duties.
- **Corps of Provincial Artificers:** Formed in March 1813 to assist the regular Royal Engineers in Upper Canada, this unit was also known as the Coloured Corps because all its members were free blacks.

Indian Territory: In 1812, this land was mostly unsettled and was defended by just a few forts, so very few military units were raised from it. The only 'white' inhabitants of the Indian Territory were *voyageurs* (hunters) and fur traders, who were partly regularized in order to serve in military corps. Coming from the upper Mississippi Valley, the British/Canadian forces were soon able to capture northern Michigan and Wisconsin from the Americans and kept the initiative in this theatre of operations for most of the War of 1812. In July 1814, some Francophone *voyageurs* were recruited in the Indian Territory in order to form volunteer companies: these became known as the Mississippi Volunteers and initially consisted of just one company with sixty-five men. Apparently, this volunteer corps also comprised a small detachment of artillery.

Nova Scotia: The general militia of the colony consisted of twenty-six infantry battalions, known by the name of the county in which they were formed. Some of these had attached artillery companies. The city of Halifax, the capital of Nova Scotia, deployed one volunteer company of artillery.

New Brunswick: Saint John, the colony's capital, had one company of volunteer artillery.

The West Indies

By the end of the eighteenth century, the islands collectively known as the West Indies – located in the Caribbean – were economically one of the most profitable areas of the world. Having been colonized by the European powers for many years, they produced large amounts of sugar that was sold around the globe at very high prices. In addition, albeit on a smaller scale, they produced other very profitable crops such as indigo and coffee. Several of these islands were colonies of Great Britain, and represented about one-third of the country's foreign trade. Thanks to the direct taxes and duties coming from the Caribbean colonies, Britain was able to become the most important of the colonial powers during the eighteenth century. Consequently, it was absolutely vital for the Crown to protect such a lucrative portion of the ever-expanding British Empire. This became particularly true when, with the outbreak of the Revolutionary Wars, the British West Indies started to be menaced by the French (who had their own flourishing colonies in the Caribbean). Operating in the West Indies, however, was not a simple matter for the British Army: the tropical climate was unsustainable for European troops, who were frequently decimated by terrible tropical fevers. British soldiers thus preferred avoiding service in the West Indies due to the unhealthy local living conditions. To solve this problem and to garrison the Crown's possessions in that part of the world, the British Army had no choice but to raise an increasing number of military units from the local communities of free blacks. These were accustomed to the climate and temperatures of the Caribbean, and thus could easily live in that theatre of operations. Until 1793, the British military garrison of the West Indies had been entirely made up of white regular regiments, which were sent to the Caribbean for periods of service before being transferred to other areas of

Officer of the Royal Engineers with M1812 dress. Note that the lapels of the tunic are worn with the coloured side on the front.

the empire. Then, in October 1793, the first of several new black units was formed, this being a Corps of Black Military Artificers and Pioneers. Mostly recruited from ex-criminals who had been freed, it comprised 300 pioneers and 100 artificers. This unit was followed by several others, including two corps of Colonial Marines (naval infantrymen) that were raised from free blacks. A First Corps of Colonial Marines (150 men) existed between 1808 and 1810, while a Second Corps (three companies, gradually expanded to six) was active from 1814–1816. Since most of the white Royal Marines were involved in the military operations taking place in Europe, the Royal Navy badly needed some local naval infantry for service in the Caribbean. In addition to those mentioned above, the British deployed the following cavalry and artillery units in the Caribbean:

- **Royal Dutch Artillery:** When the British occupied the Dutch colony of Surinam in 1799, the local white garrison was taken into British pay. It was reorganized as an infantry battalion known as the Royal Dutch Battalion and as two artillery companies, the Royal Dutch Artillery. In December 1802, when Surinam was returned to the Dutch, these units were transferred back to the Dutch Army. In 1804, when the British occupied Surinam for the second time, the local white troops were reorganized as the Surinam Chasseurs.
- **Independent Companies of Foreign Artillery:** This corps was created in 1798 by assembling the artillery companies of two mercenary units that had been sent for service in the West Indies. Most of their soldiers were German, while a good number of the officers were French royalists. In 1803, the two companies were disbanded and absorbed into a newly created Royal Foreign Artillery corps which comprised a total of three companies. The latter were all disbanded in 1817.

The British colonies in the West Indies also had their local units of militia, which were made up of all the able-bodied white colonists living on their territory as well as of the free blacks who were available for military service. Generally speaking, the white settlers served in cavalry units or as officers for the infantry formations, while the free blacks made up the rank-and-file of the foot units. Like in Canada, the militiamen were required to provide their own uniforms and personal equipment; in addition, they had to train on a regular basis, at least once a month. In case of emergency, the militia could be augmented with the inclusion of slaves, but the latter could not be armed with firearms (they received only pikes). All the British militias organized in the Caribbean area were also to act as policing forces, since slave uprisings took place regularly. One of their primary tasks was to chase maroons and runaway slaves in order to keep order in the plantations.

Antigua: The militia of this colony at the beginning of the nineteenth century comprised several units. These consisted of two infantry regiments, one independent infantry company, one squadron of dragoons and one battalion of artillery.

Bahamas: Each of the islands making up the Bahamas archipelago had its own militia units. Nassau could count on one infantry regiment with 500 men, one troop of light dragoons and one artillery company made up of volunteers. Crooked Island had one infantry and one artillery company, while Exuma and Long Island each had one infantry company.

Barbados: This colony had quite a large militia, comprising one infantry regiment for each of the eleven parishes that made up the territory of Barbados. In addition to these, which consisted of some 3,330 militiamen including 400 free blacks, there was a small cavalry unit of 60 troopers known as Life Guards.

Grenada: The militia of this island, mustering 1,200 men, consisted of five infantry regiments plus one troop of light dragoons and two companies of artillery. A smaller nearby island, part of the same colony, had its own independent infantry regiment.

Jamaica: This colony had the largest militia of all the British territories in the West Indies, consisting of around 8,000 men and including at least 3,000 free blacks. They were organized on eighteen infantry regiments, three regiments of cavalry (one for each county) and several artillery companies. Temporary companies were occasionally formed from local natives and loyal maroons, in order to combat the illegal activities of the runaway slaves in the woods.

Saint Vincent: This British possession had two regiments and five independent companies of infantry, as well as one troop of cavalry and one company of artillery.

Tobago: In 1803, the militia of this colony was reorganized to comprise one infantry regiment with nine companies, one troop of cavalry and one company of artillery.

Trinidad: This British territory had a quite large and well-organized militia consisting of three regiments and eight independent companies of infantry, one regiment of light dragoons, one regiment of hussars, three corps of mounted chasseurs and one brigade of artillery. One of the infantry regiments, the Royal Trinidad Infantry, and the various cavalry units were made up of just white settlers, while the other corps mostly comprised free blacks who were under the orders of white officers.

Soldier of the Royal Staff Corps with M1800 uniform.

South Africa

In 1806, the British expanded their small colonial possessions in Africa by capturing the Cape of Good Hope (South Africa) from the Dutch. This colony was located in a strategic position, since it controlled the most significant commercial and naval routes connecting the Atlantic Ocean with the Pacific. For this reason, it had to be well garrisoned. The Dutch East India Company had established a permanent military garrison at the Cape of Good Hope since the closing decades of the eighteenth century. In 1793, this consisted of just one unit recruited from the local Hottentots and known as the Pandour Corps, which numbered only 200 soldiers. In 1795, the British first occupied the Cape of Good Hope, and during the following year they reorganized the Pandour Corps as the new Hottentot Corps, now with 300 men. In 1801, the corps was expanded to become a regiment with ten companies, which was designated as the Cape Regiment. Following the signing of the Peace of Amiens with France, the Cape of Good Hope was returned to the Dutch, who maintained in service the Cape Regiment but changed its denomination twice during the following years (first renaming it as the Corps of Free Hottentots and later as the Hottentot Light Infantry). In 1806, the British conquered the Cape of Good Hope permanently and thus reorganized the Cape Regiment. This was now to have ten companies, whose officers and NCOs were all white, while the rank and file were recruited from the Hottentots. The original unit was later expanded with the addition of a light cavalry troop. In 1817, the bulk of the Cape Regiment was disbanded; the cavalry troop, however, was retained in service, and was reorganized in 1827 to form the famous Cape Mounted Rifles.

Australia

In 1787, the famous First Fleet departed from Portsmouth to found a penal colony in Australia. This was to be the first permanent settlement of the new British colony, which had been discovered by James Cook only in 1770 and which started to become important for the Crown only after the Thirteen Colonies were lost due to the American Revolution. To guard the convicts transported on the First Fleet and to garrison the future penal colony, a unit known as the New South Wales Marine Corps was formed. This consisted of 160 Royal Marines (organized in four companies) who volunteered for service in Australia, a territory which at the time was known as New South Wales. The New South Wales Marine Corps acted as the sole garrison of Australia until 1791/1792, when the New South Wales Corps was formed. This new unit started to be raised in Britain in 1789 as a regular infantry corps that would make up the permanent garrison of New South Wales. It initially consisted of just

Civilian contractor of the Artillery Train in 1792 dress.

300 soldiers in three companies; the small size of this establishment can be explained by the fact that very few British soldiers were willing to serve in such a distant and little-known colonial outpost. After arriving in Australia, the corps was expanded to four companies thanks to the enlistment of 100 former members of the New South Wales Marines who had decided to remain in Australia.

India

The British presence in India had started to be a significant one since the middle of the eighteenth century after the Battle of Plassey, that was fought in 1757. Until then, other European colonial powers such as France and Portugal had been exerting a greater influence over India than had Britain. Since the first territorial acquisitions in the Indian subcontinent, the British government had not annexed any Indian territory as a direct possession of the Crown; the British territories in India were all under control of the East India Company. The Company, established in 1600, was a joint-stock venture that originally had as its main objective that of trading with the rich countries of the Asian continent. Like its Dutch equivalent operating in present-day Indonesia, the British East India Company gradually emerged as a regional power in Asia and expanded its commercial influence by using political and military measures. Over time, the British traders started to occupy several important cities in India as well as variouss tracts of coastline. All these new territories were to act as outposts for the economic activities of the Company, and were also centres from which the British could exert their influence over the local Indian rulers. By the middle of the eighteenth century, with the decline of the great Moghul Empire, India was fractioned into a multitude of independent princedoms. These had outdated armies using traditional Indian weaponry and tactics, which were no match for the modern military technologies employed by the British. As a result, the East India Company gradually used its great resources to transform several of the Indian native states into protectorates. Thanks to the signing of favourable treaties concerning trade, the British acquired direct control over an increasing number of cities and territories. After the great victory at Plassey, after which the French were expelled from most of India, the British could expand their possessions towards the interior of the subcontinent.

Consequently, during the following decades, the East India Company was forced to reorganize its military forces: these initially very small units had the main task of protecting the commercial interests of the Company and garrisoning its territorial possessions. From their foundation, the military forces of the Company included a certain number of native soldiers, recruited with the help of local rulers who were allies of the Company and making up a private military organization that was not part of the British Army. On many occasions, the European and native components of the East India Company's forces cooperated very well together and showed great efficiency on the field of battle. With the reorganization that followed Plassey, they also started to have significant numbers and their standards of service became comparable to those of contemporary European armies. The Company's military units could be European, made up of soldiers from Britain, or native corps recruited from the local population but having British officers. The Indian soldiers serving European rulers, be they Hindus or Muslims, were commonly known as sepoys. Generally speaking, the European soldiers recruited by the Company in Britain were not of the same quality as those who served in the regular British Army, which offered better conditions of service to potential recruits and thus the best elements wishing to serve in the military usually entered the ranks of the regulars. Most of the British soldiers serving under the flags of the Company were individuals who had decided to leave their country in search of an opportunity, and who lived at the margins of their home society. Some of them had experienced problems with justice, while others had no choice but to enlist as soldiers of fortune in order to earn a living. The members of the European military units, however, also comprised significant numbers of whites who were recruited in India from all the European adventurers or mercenaries who were in search of employment. French, Swiss, German and Dutch recruits were the most common to find, but there were also individuals of mixed ancestry (half-European and half-Indian). While these soldiers' discipline and training were not the same as their equivalents serving in the British Army, on most occasions they proved to be reliable fighters.

At the beginning of the nineteenth century, the territorial possessions of the British East India Company were organized into three autonomous presidencies: Madras, Bengal and Bombay. Each of these had its own army, comprising several military units. Generally speaking, the armies of the three presidencies were mostly made up of infantry and included only a limited number of cavalry. However, the few mounted troops could be of good quality, despite usually having a semi-regular status. They were all native units, commanded by British officers. In Bengal, the regular cavalry of the East India Company consisted of eight regiments, all designated as light cavalry. In addition, there were a Governor General's Bodyguard, formed by picked officers and men taken from the ordinary regiments, and some regiments of irregular native cavalry. The latter were recruited using the sillidar system, according to which local horsemen were to independently provide and maintain their own horses and equipment. In Madras, the regular cavalry consisted of eight light cavalry regiments, while those in Bombay comprised just one troop of horse. The armies of the three

Soldier of the Royal Artillery Drivers with pre-1811 dress.

presidencies also included some units of artillery and engineers, whose members were all European and which had an excellent reputation (being considered practically of the same level as their British Army equivalents). Bengal had three troops of horse artillery and three battalions of foot artillery, while Madras had two troops of horse artillery and three battalions of foot artillery, and Bombay had one troop of horse artillery and two battalions of foot artillery. Each of the three presidencies had its own Engineer Corps, consisting of a small number of British officers having specific technical competencies. These officers were at the head of a labour force consisting of sappers, who were recruited from the local Indian communities. There were two sapper companies in Bengal, while Bombay and Madras had one company each.

In 1796, the British captured the Dutch colony of Ceylon (modern Sri Lanka), a large island located to the south of India. Similarly to what happened in Surinam or South Africa, the local Dutch military garrison was transferred to British pay. The independent companies of Malays that had been serving under the Dutch were consolidated into a larger unit, known as the 1st Ceylon Regiment in 1801. During the following year, another regiment of this kind was organized for service in Sri Lanka. In 1805, a 3rd Ceylon Regiment was created, followed by a 4th Regiment in 1810. In October 1804, the British also organized a corps of Ceylon Light Dragoons, mostly raised from sepoys serving in the Madras army of the East India Company. This had an establishment of 130 men, forty of whom were British. From 1801, the British also raised three companies of gun lascars for service in Ceylon, these being native

NCO of the Royal Artillery Drivers with M1811 uniform.

transporters who were essential for the Royal Artillery. Most of these soldiers came from Bengal. In 1804, three companies of pioneer lascars were also formed. In 1811, following the annexation of the Netherlands to the French Empire, an Anglo-Indian military force occupied the Dutch East Indies (present-day Indonesia). To patrol the large territory of Java, the most important island of the Dutch East Indies, two cavalry squadrons were raised in India in 1812. These were known as the Java Hussars and were disbanded only in 1816, when Indonesia was returned to the Netherlands.

Chapter 7

Royal Marines, Royal Marine Artillery and Sea Fencibles

Until 1755, the naval infantry component of the Royal Navy was provided by several infantry regiments that were detached for sea service from the rest of the British Army. This practice of using normal infantry units to perform naval infantry duties had begun in 1664, when the famous Duke of York and Albany's Maritime Regiment of Foot was raised. This unit, also known as the Admiral's Regiment, provided infantrymen to several warships of the English Navy. In 1755, the British government decided to organize an independent corps of naval infantry, which received the official denomination of Marines (this was changed to Royal Marines only in 1802). The new naval infantrymen were initially structured on fifteen autonomous companies, each of which could be sent to serve on one warship. Unlike the sailors of the Royal Navy, the Marines were all volunteers like the infantry of the army, and thus had a lot in common with them (including their uniform). The various companies of Marines were assembled, at least from an administrative point of view, into three divisions that took their name from the location where they were based: Chatham, Portsmouth and Plymouth. In 1805, a fourth division was established at Woolwich. By that date, the general organization of the Royal Marines was as follows: forty-seven companies in the Chatham Division, forty-eight companies in the Portsmouth Division, the same number in the Plymouth Division and thirty companies in the Woolwich Division. Each company comprised the following elements: one captain, two first lieutenants, two second lieutenants, eight sergeants, eight corporals, five drummers and 130 privates (increased to 140 in 1808). By December 1815, the total number of companies had been gradually reduced to 80. Until 1804, each of the three divisions that existed at that time also comprised one company of grenadiers and one of light infantry, but these were later transformed into ordinary companies. The Royal Marines played a key role during the Napoleonic Wars, and on several occasions supported the British Army by fighting as normal line infantry. Their main tasks, however, were acting as marksmen on warships, conducting boarding operations, manning the guns of the warships on which they served and organizing amphibious landings. In addition, they had to prevent or crush any mutinies that might take place among the sailors of a warship.

Trooper of the Staff Corps of Cavalry.

In 1810, a 1st Battalion of Marines was formed by assembling together six companies; a 2nd Battalion was created in July 1812, also with six companies, and a 3rd Battalion (with ten companies) was added in January 1814. These were specifically created to operate in North America, in the War of 1812 that was fought against the USA. The first two battalions arrived in North America in June 1813, while the latter was sent to fight against the Americans only in June 1814. In May 1814, shortly before the arrival of the 3rd Battalion, the 2nd Battalion was broken up and its men were assigned to other functions. As a result, the former 3rd Battalion became the new 2nd Battalion, and a new 3rd Battalion was formed by merging two

Trooper of the Staff Corps of Cavalry.

Royal Marine wearing M1802 dress.

existing corps of Colonial Marines. The First Corps of Colonial Marines was formed in 1808, while the Second Corps was raised in 1814; both units were made up of free blacks (former slaves) who came from British possessions in the West Indies. Since most of the regular Royal Marines were involved in the military operations fought in Europe, the British authorities decided to raise a number of blacks for service on warships operating in the Caribbean. The new 3rd Battalion of Royal Marines formed from the Colonial Marines was disbanded in 1815, when hostilities with the USA came to an end. Until 1804, the guns of the Royal Navy's warships were manned by the Marines or by the sailors embarked on each vessel; this, however, sometimes caused serious difficulties, since a specific level of competence was needed to fire the naval guns of a warship effectively. As a result, in August of that year, a new corps known as the Royal Marine Artillery was formed. This was part of the Royal Marines, but its members were naval artillerymen and not naval infantry. Each of the four divisions of Royal Marines had one company of Royal Marine Artillery, with a single company comprising the following elements: one captain, three first lieutenants, five second lieutenants, eight sergeants, five corporals, eight bombardiers, three drummers and sixty-two gunners.

There were also the Sea Fencibles, the maritime equivalent of the Fencibles, whose units were discussed in a previous chapter. The Sea Fencibles were a sort of maritime 'home guard', based at the coastal towns of Britain and tasked with defending the coastline from enemy incursions. Their duties also included manning coastal batteries and patrolling the local coastline with small boats. Most of them were fishermen during civil life and served on a part-time basis, although they were led by commissioned officers provided by the Royal Navy. Raised in 1798, the Sea Fencibles consisted of thirty-six independent companies; each of them tasked with defending a specific sector of the British coastline. Interestingly, the city of London had an independent Corps of River Fencibles that operated on the Thames during the Napoleonic era. In 1810, all the companies of Sea Fencibles were disbanded, after having seen action on several occasions during the previous years.

Uniforms and equipment

As the Royal Marines were always dressed in red, like the line infantry of the British Army, they were given the nickname of 'Lobsters' by the sailors who served with them on the warships of the Royal Navy. The uniform worn until 1802 was as follows: black bicorn with white external edge and black cockade, red long-tailed coat with white collar and round cuffs, white shoulder straps, white frontal lapels, white waistcoat and trousers, black gaiters and white leather belt equipment. In

1802, a new dress was adopted, which remained unchanged until the end of the Napoleonic Wars: black round hat with white band wrapped around the bottom part and white-and-red plume, red single-breasted jacket with dark blue collar and round cuffs, white piping to the collar, additional white lace on the buttonholes of the jacket's front and of the cuffs, dark blue shoulder straps with white piping and white crest, white trousers, black gaiters and white leather belt equipment. The Royal Marine Artillery was dressed very similarly to the Foot Artillery: black round hat with brass frontal plate, black cockade and white plume, dark blue single-breasted jacket with red collar and round cuffs piped in yellow, red shoulder straps piped in yellow, additional yellow lace on the buttonholes of the jacket's front and cuffs, dark blue trousers, black gaiters and white leather belt equipment. On campaign, the round cap was replaced by a dark blue fatigue cap, and a simpler version of the jacket (without piping and additional lace on the buttonholes) was worn. The Sea Fencibles had no uniforms to speak of.

Bibliography

Barnes, R.M., *A History of the Regiments and Uniforms of the British Army* (Seeley Service, 1950)

Chappell, M., *Redcaps: Britain's Military Police* (Osprey Publishing, 1997)

Chappell, M., *The King's German Legion 1803–1812* (Osprey Publishing, 2000)

Chappell, M., *The King's German Legion 1812–1816* (Osprey Publishing, 2000)

Chappell, M., *Wellington's Peninsula Regiments: The Irish* (Osprey Publishing, 2003)

Chartrand, R., *A Scarlet Coat: Uniforms, Flags and Equipment of the British Forces in the War of 1812* (Service Publications, 2011)

Chartrand, R., *British Forces in North America 1793–1815* (Osprey Publishing, 1998)

Chartrand, R., *British Forces in the West Indies 1793–1815* (Osprey Publishing, 1996)

Chartrand, R., *Emigré and Foreign Troops in British Service 1793–1803* (Osprey Publishing, 1999)

Chartrand, R., *Emigré and Foreign Troops in British Service 1803–1815* (Osprey Publishing, 2000)

Esposito, G., *Armies of the War of 1812: United States, United Kingdom and Canada 1812–1815* (Winged Hussar Publishing, 2017)

Fosten, B., *Wellington's Heavy Cavalry* (Osprey Publishing, 1982)

Fosten, B., *Wellington's Light Cavalry* (Osprey Publishing, 1982)

Franklin, C.E., *British Napoleonic Uniforms* (The History Press, 2008)

Haythornthwaite, P., *British Cavalryman 1792–1815* (Osprey Publishing, 1994)

Haythornthwaite, P., *Nelson's Navy* (Osprey Publishing, 1993)

Haythornthwaite, P., *The Armies of Wellington* (Arms and Armour Press, 1994)

Haythornthwaite, P., *Uniforms of the Peninsular War 1807–1814* (Blandford Press, 1978)

Haythornthwaite, P., *Uniforms of Waterloo in Colour* (Blandford Press, 1974)

Haythornthwaite, P., *Wellington's Army: the Uniforms of the British Soldier 1812–1815* (Greenhill Books, 2002)

Haythornthwaite, P., *Wellington's Specialist Troops* (Osprey Publishing, 1988)

Hofschroer, P., *The Hanoverian Army of the Napoleonic Wars* (Osprey Publishing, 1989)

Katcher, P., *The American War 1812–1814* (Osprey Publishing, 1990)

Lawson, Cecil C.P., *A History of the Uniforms of the British Army* (Littlehampton Book Services, 1974)

Reid, S., *Armies of the East India Company 1750–1850* (Osprey Publishing, 2009)

Windrow, M., *Military Dress of the Peninsular War 1808–1814* (Hippocrene Books, 1975)

Index